Bible Wonderings

1, Reason
2, Faith

Also by Donald Schmidt:

God's Paintbrush Celebration Kit *(with Rabbi Sandy Eisenberg Sasso)*

Emerging Word: a Creation Spirituality Lectionary

Bible Wonderings

✦

Familiar Tales Retold

Donald Schmidt

iUniverse, Inc.

New York Lincoln Shanghai

Bible Wonderings
Familiar Tales Retold

Copyright © 2006 by Donald Schmidt

iUniverse books may be ordered through booksellers or by contacting:

iUniverse
2021 Pine Lake Road, Suite 100
Lincoln, NE 68512
www.iuniverse.com
1-800-Authors (1-800-288-4677)

ISBN-13: 978-0-595-40311-0 (pbk)
ISBN-13: 978-0-595-84687-0 (ebk)
ISBN-10: 0-595-40311-5 (pbk)
ISBN-10: 0-595-84687-4 (ebk)

Printed in the United States of America

The stories *Sarah's Laughter; Plans and Possibilities (Joseph and Benjamin);* and *Running from God (Elijah)* have previously appeared in *The Whole People of God.* The stories *Plans and Possibilities (Joseph and Benjamin)* and *John the Baptist and the Brood of Vipers* have previously appeared in *Seasons of the Spirit.* They are reprinted here with permission of Wood Lake Books.

The photograph on the front cover shows a stained glass window in the Nahiku Congregational Church (United Church of Christ) in the village of Nahiku on the island of Maui, Hawai'i. The window, depicting the cross amidst a variety of Hawaiian flowers, is the work of Maui artist Wayne Sprinkler and was donated to the church by the late George Harrison and his wife Olivia Harrison. The image is used by kind permission of Rev. Cynthia Allencastre.

The illustrations of Hawaiian flowers throughout the book are by Fred Lorenzo.

Contents

Acknowledgements

Several people read various stories over the years as they were forming and provided vital feedback, much of which has found its way onto these pages. I especially need to thank Carolyn Pogue, John Indermark, and Lorna Kelly.

I also have to give thanks to Don whose support, encouragement, and insights made the completion of this book possible. *Mahalo nui loa.*

Ways to use this book

Read it

It is a storybook. You can simply put your feet up, sit back, and enjoy it.

Use it for personal study and spiritual growth

If you want to go one step further, you can use the study guide at the back for personal reflection. There are general suggestions, as well as specific questions for each story.

Group Bible study

The study guide can also be used by small groups for discussion and exploration. Follow the guidelines, and adapt it to suit the purposes and desires of your group. You may wish to work all the way through the book, or choose a few stories for a short study: for example, *Magnificat*, the two *John the Baptist* pieces, and *A Child Is Born* would make a good Advent study.

Or, *Dear Jesus, Born Again?*, the two *Prodigal* stories, and *Pilate's Report* would make a good Lenten study, ending up with *Mary Magdalene's Legacy* after Easter.

Try a six-week study on women, or men, or parables, or…use your imagination.

Worship

Several of the stories lend themselves to being read in worship, either directly or, with minor adaptation, as dramatic readings. A lectionary index is provided to indicate where the stories fall during the liturgical year in various lectionaries.

Introduction

"Tell me the old, old, story…"

"Tell me the stories of Jesus…"

"I love to tell the story…"

"We are a people of a story…"

Funny, I can't think off-hand of a single hymn that begins "Let's reminisce about the laws of Leviticus…" or "Sing to me once again the census figures of Nehemiah…"

That's not an accident. I think, when all is said and done, most of us view the Bible as a storybook.

By that I don't mean to say that I think we view it as fiction. What I mean to say is that, more than anything else, it tells a story. God's story. Our story.

And that story is so very, very important. It may be ancient, but it is as relevant today as it has ever been.

From early childhood, I have loved the stories of the Bible. We had Bible storybooks in our home. We went to Sunday School (every week, rain or shine!) and learned stories. The ones I remember the most are the ones I could "see." Not necessarily in a picture, but stories told in such a way that I could imagine them being real, could place myself in them, could wonder about them afterwards.

Over the years, as I have read the Bible and engaged it as a preacher and a writer and an educator, I have found myself inside the stories—not always by choice. Sometimes they just grab me, even when I'm not looking. A character asks me a question, and all day long I'm struggling with it. Or I imagine an event and wonder why it turned out a certain way.

Why *did* the Syro-Phoenician woman confront Jesus that particular way on that particular day? Don't you wonder why God preferred Abel's offering to Cain's? What do you suppose Lydia and Paul talked about when she pressed him to stay at her home?

Sometimes the questions are less profound, but no less real. As a child I struggled for quite some time with this one: When God prepares a table before me in the presence of my enemies, what kind of food is on the table? I needed to know because what if there was going to be a food fight? That may seem silly now, but it was a very important—and practical—question at the time.

All of this is to remember that, of course, there are no wrong questions (or wrong answers, either).

We need to open ourselves to wonder more about stories, especially biblical ones. Taking them at face value can be okay, but we can learn and gain so much more from them when we allow ourselves to wonder, to question, to play "what if?" with them a little. It helps to approach them from a different direction, and to let them challenge us.

Christian educator and friend Susan Burt puts it well: "When we exercise our imaginative spirit, we move the biblical story out of literalism, factuality, certainty, and fixed answers, and into the unknown. The story is born anew—a liberating, healing story, revealing deep truths, and an invitation to discern God's message for this time."[1]

The stories in this book are an experiment in just that—using the imaginative spirit to unlock biblical stories from their moorings, at least temporarily, and let them float for a little while, so we might look at them from a different angle.

In most cases, I have taken as my starting point one small textual "twist" and expanded on it, just for the sake of wondering. For example, in the case of the Zacchaeus story, an alternative translation of one word can change the story considerably. Doesn't make it better or worse, just differ-

---

1.   In Mike Schwartzentruber, ed., *The Emerging Christian Way: Thoughts, Stories, and Wisdom for a Faith of Transformation*, (Kelowna, BC: Copper House, 2006), p. 216.

ent. In some of the other cases, I've simply sought to change the context for the sake of seeing things in a fresh way.

In every instance, these are mere moments frozen in a microsecond of time. They're snapshots from my literary imagination. They are not meant to be definitive, they're just meant to be stories. One person's stories. I hope they inspire your own.

Donald Schmidt
Lahaina, Maui, Hawai'i
www.emergingword.com

Sarah's Laughter

Scripture reference: Genesis 18:1–15, 21:1–7

Was Sarah really all that thrilled to learn about becoming pregnant at the age of 90? One has to wonder just what her feelings were as she prepared to give birth to the child that she and Abraham named "Laughter."

Laugh?
You bet I laughed.

A deep, disgusted,
        confused, frustrated,
        angry laugh,
And Abraham laughed, too,
        don't forget that.

Imagine: pregnant at my age!
All those years of longing
     praying
     hoping
     dreaming
for what? nothing!
More wandering in deserts
     of barrenness
     and loneliness.
More nasty remarks from the neighbors:
     "Oh how sad,
     there goes poor Sarah,
     barren all these years.
     Makes you wonder
what sin she's paying for…"

And then to be told
this appalling joke: pregnant at 90!
     What could I do but laugh?
Crying's quite out of the question
     with something so ludicrous as this.

But then reality—and the anger—
     set in.

Why now, God?
Why after all these years?
What's the point?
I've never known you to be this cruel.

I asked,
begged—
     okay, demanded sometimes,
but yearned,

longed,
pined,
cried out…
 "Why didn't you hear me, God?
Why?"

And yet
 after the initial shock
we thought:
 why not now?

God has always been surprising us,
shocking us,
pushing the limits just a little more each time,
inviting us to trust
in new and unusual ways.
 Was this really any different
 from all the other challenges?

I remember the night
after the messengers came.
Abraham had a little too much to drink
and crawled into my tent
rather sheepishly,
almost like a nervous youth.

He made some silly remark
about needing to sleep with me—
 how it was God's will—
and we laughed and loved into the night.

And when it all came true,
I was horrified.
 All of the joy I had once had,

the dreams of giving birth,
        gave way to deathly fear.

Yet Abraham held me close,
and we cried and questioned together,
and wondered,
and
wondered.

No small eternity later
        Isaac was born,
and I whose dreams had all but dried up
        held that bundle of hope and promise
        to my breast.

And as I watched Abraham hold him aloft
        proud beyond words
I was overcome with joy
        and thanksgiving
for a God so full of surprises.

Laugh?
You bet I laughed.

Plans and Possibilities

(Joseph and Benjamin)

Scripture reference: Genesis 45:15–21

Often I hear people say "it's all a part of God's plan" and I wonder just what they mean. So I thought about the story of Joseph and his brothers—one of the longest stories in the Bible—and how Joseph ends by telling his brothers that God had a plan in all of it. But is a plan the same thing as a script? Does God decide in advance exactly how things are going to go, or does God have a hope, a dream, of how things will unfold, and then work with our free will, which sometimes can go in the strangest directions?

Two men sat at the river's edge, dangling their feet in the cool water. While a close look might have suggested that they were brothers, you would have been forgiven for wondering what in the world they had in common. One was rugged, earth-worn, and tired from hard work; the other showed signs of stress that had been compensated for many times over with the trappings of fine living.

"So, tell me what things have been like since I left," the finer-looking one asked.

"It's not been easy," the other replied. "Father never really recovered from your death—I mean, what he thought was your death. He tried to put on a brave face, but at night I would hear him wail, tossing and turning in his bed. Sometimes, when it was just the two of us, he'd give me a hug for no reason and almost shudder at his own words. 'Dear Benjamin,' he'd say, 'you're all that's left to me of my beloved Rachel. She was the fairest flower of all the field, and now she's gone.' And as if I hadn't heard the story a hundred times already, he would recount how our mother had died giving birth to me, and how he had unconsciously blamed me for her death, and how he thought that was why God had taken you from him, to teach him a lesson, that he might come to love me more."

"Oh Ben, Ben—you mustn't blame yourself. God doesn't work that way."

"I'd like to believe that, I really would. But it's hard sometimes."

"I know."

They sat in silence a minute, casually tossing pebbles into the river. Then Joseph continued:

"I mean, look at all I've gone through; do you think I deserved it?"

"Of course not!"

"Or do you think God planned it all?"

"Well, no, but…you yourself said that God had a plan."

"A plan, yes…"

"So, what's the difference?"

"Do I think God had a plan to help feed people during this time of famine? Yes. Do I think that that's why our dear brothers threw me down a well, or why Potiphar had me thrown in jail? No."

"I don't understand."

"I've had time to think. Trust me, Ben, the life I've had, I've had a *lot* of time to think. And to reflect. And to try to make sense of everything that's happened. The thing is: I *can't* make sense of it. Not in the least. But I can see the hand of God in all of it, Ben."

Joseph tossed another rock into the river, this time with intent and purpose, and it skipped three times before it gave in to the depths.

"We make our own decisions, Ben. Sometimes good ones, sometimes bad ones. But God takes the consequences of our actions and tries to work with what we offer. So you guys threw me in a pit and sold me for a slave. On the one hand, I was an arrogant little so and so—I'll admit it. But on the other hand, it wasn't my idea to be Dad's favorite. And on the other hand still, considering how Dad and Uncle Esau grew up…you see why I can't make sense of it. But God can.

"God can make sense of all our foolishness, our pride, our stubbornness. And God can work through it—despite it, I dare say—and somehow try to give us a silver lining. It doesn't always work out that way. Yet sometimes it does, even when we can't see it for all of the pain that still clutters our lives.

"But sometimes we can: we can look back and see the hand of God in our lives in ways that we could never have imagined at the time. Sometimes we can say, 'I'm glad things turned out how they did.' Maybe that's the best we can ever hope for in this life."

Torah Talk

(Moses)

Scripture reference: Exodus 20:1–17; Deuteronomy 5:1–21

The joyous sense of God's law as a guide or way (a more literal translation of the Hebrew word torah) *is something that we Christians seem to have lost. The sense of law being described as "sweeter than honeycomb" in Psalm 19 is a beautiful part of our heritage. Yet we tend to have a sense that God's law, like human laws, is there to restrict us and frustrate us. God repeatedly offers to humankind ways to salvation and new life, not stumbling blocks set to trip us up. Why do we always seem to get it wrong?*

"Moses!"

The shout thundered through the camp. Everyone began to search. "Where is he?" "Moses, where are you?" "I saw him a minute ago." The shout came again, this time even louder: "Moses!!"

He stumbled out of his tent, struggling with his clothing.

A woman ran towards him, "Hurry up, hurry up. You're…'wanted' and as she spoke she pointed her thumb in the direction of the mountaintop.

"Moses!!!"

"You'd better hurry."

Fumbling with his belt, Moses began the climb, scrambling over the rocks in a rush of fear and fury.

"What could he possibly want this time?" Moses wondered as he climbed. "And why the urgency? Have we done something wrong…again? Have *I* done something wrong?"

"Moses!!!!"

The whole mountain shook, and a thick cloud of smoke (or maybe it was just fog?) floated down the mountainside.

"I'm coming, Lord," Moses shouted back. He wanted to mutter "hold your horses" under his breath but thought better of it.

Moses reached the top, quite out of breath, and dusted himself off. He was surprised to find a man standing a little nervously beside a table.

"Sit down, Moses, sit down," the man said.

"Is it…you?"

"Yes, Moses, it's me. I thought if we were going to talk you might feel a little less intimidated if I spoke as one of you, so here I am."

Moses sat down—puzzled, but relieved at the apparent conciliatory mood. His host paced back and forth, slightly agitated, but hesitant.

"The thing is, Moses, I've been thinking."

"Yes?"

"I'm worried about the people. I'm worried about the direction they're going."

"Well, perhaps, once we, I mean, when…I think, well, the thing is…All of the other nations have laws. We just haven't had much time—you know how it's been since we left Egypt, all of the traveling, the food and water thing, all of that. Once we get settled, establish ourselves, I think we'll be fine."

"That's just it, you see. I've thought about it long and hard," God said. "All the other nations are established and have laws. And where does that lead them? Into getting stuck in their ways, and into breaking their laws, and into making more laws to pile on top of others. It's a vicious cycle. I want better for my people."

"Well, you know how we're always open to suggestions." Moses tried a smile and even a little laugh but it didn't come off very well. He continued, "What exactly did you have in mind?"

God sat down, and took a deep breath.

"I was thinking: what if I gave my people some guidelines, some direction?"

"With all due respect," Moses offered, "I'm not sure I understand the difference."

"Oh, there's a lot of difference. Laws are rigid, no room to breathe. They inspire dishonesty and cheating. People know that if they don't do something, they'll be punished, so their whole manner of living becomes one of avoiding punishment, not of doing the right thing.

"No," God continued, "I want my people to live differently. I want them to do the right thing simply because it's right, not just to keep their backsides out of the fire, if you catch my drift."

"What sort of guidelines are you thinking of?" Moses asked.

"Well, some general suggestions for behavior. How to treat each other, how to find happiness in life, how to live in harmony with each other, and with all the rest of my beautiful creation."

"Sounds good to me. Where do we begin?"

"I think you should begin by remembering," God said. "Remember me. Remember that I created you from the dust of the earth, breathed life into you—*my* life—and that I listened to you when you cried out in pain and anguish, when you were slaves in Egypt.

"I want you to remember that *I* am the one who rescued you, and brought you into a new life. And that I'll keep doing that, too, I promise. I keep my promises. I'm not going to give up on you. But I need you to cooperate. I can't keep my end of the bargain very well if you go off trying to do your own thing all of the time.

"I need you to worship me. Respect me. Love me. Pay attention to me. Remember, I am alive, and I want to be in relationship with you. Times and things will change, Moses, and I'll be there for you, I promise. Trust me. I will not let you down.

"But if you go swarming off after some new-fangled, bigger and better so-called god, I won't be responsible. Do you understand that? You can't have two gods at once—it doesn't work. I'll always be here, I'm not going anywhere. But when you go chasing whatever turns your crank because it's flashy at the time, you lose sight of me, and you're on your own. Because…" (he stood up and started pacing again) "it hurts when you do that. There, I've said it, you've seen my weakness. It just plain hurts when my people reject me.

"I love them, care for them. When Rachel fell and broke her leg on the walk the other day, I cried, too. And when Ben's lamb died, I felt sad. When you turn away from me, I hurt.

"I have feelings, Moses. And when you reject me, when you give up on me, I don't know what I can do. I will always love you, make no mistake about that. But I want you to love me in return, if we are to have a real relationship. I can't help you if you won't let me, I guess that's what I'm trying to say here." God sat down again.

"And I don't want to hear my name misused, either. People saying, 'God will get you for that!' I don't like it. That's not the way I work. Or 'May God strike me dead if I don't do this or that.' Phooey! Don't use my name unless you're talking to me, and unless you mean it."

"Okay," Moses said. "I get it."

"Now, I know you people have been traveling a long, long time, and it's been hard. Life will always be hard work. All your life, in one way or another you'll be wandering, seeking, never really arriving. That's okay—I planned it that way. To be alive is to move, to change, to grow. If you expect to feel like you've finished, you're in deep trouble. But stop and smell the flowers once in a while, for heaven's sake. Take one day a week, and stop. Just stop whatever it is you're doing day to day, and do something different. Play. Relax. Lie in the grass, go for a swim. Celebrate my creation, and renew yourself in it. That's an order.

"When you spend time enjoying creation, it will help you keep your lives in perspective. You'll remember who created it, and that you're a part of it. You'll be more inclined to thank me for it, and to take care of it.

"Now, I want you to listen to your elders. They may not always be right, but they're not always wrong, either. Take care of them, just as they took care of you when you were younger. Set a good example, and one day your children will take care of you. But more than that: listen to them. Open yourselves to their wisdom. Never underestimate the value of looking at what old eyes have already seen. You might want to look at it differently, but listen to their stories first, and then make up your mind. There is a wisdom that comes with age. Don't run away from the past, but don't stay there, either. Strike the right balance, and you'll have a long life."

Moses looked off in thought for a moment, as if he was letting it all sink in.

"Is that it?" he asked.

"Not quite. But almost. The rest is all pretty basic common sense, really. Same sorts of rules you'll find anywhere. Treat others the way you want to be treated.

"Respect one another. Don't kill, don't lie, don't cheat, don't steal. Be faithful to one another. Keep your word. Don't get hung up on having everything; you spend all your time amassing great piles of money and other things, and you'll end up empty inside, you mark my words.

"Be gentle with one another. Even when you don't want to be. And you'll go far."

There was a pause. Moses hesitated a second longer, and then ventured again, "Is *that* it?"

"Yes, I think so."

"You don't suppose you could write it down, do you? I mean, the big stuff at least, so we don't forget?"

"Oh, I don't think I'd like to do that. You write something down, and then everyone assumes it's an absolute, and they start editing it, and adding to it, and you find you're no different than anybody else. No, I don't want my people caught up in that nonsense."

"But I'm not sure I'll remember it all, and I want to tell the people exactly what you've said."

"Remember this: love me, love yourselves, love one another. You do that, and you'll make out just fine."

"Well, we can try," Moses said.

"Trying's all I ask. You take a step in my direction, I'll meet you the rest of the way. Just keep it simple—love.

God stood up. "Now, you'd better get out of here, or everyone's going to get worried about you—you know how they get."

"Thank you. Thank you so much. I'll tell them what you've said, and we'll try, we really will."

"You'll do fine. Now go on."

Running from God

(Elijah)

Scripture reference: 1 Kings 19:1–18

We all try to run from God at one time or another. Sometimes we try too hard to find God. And still other times, we do both at once.

I ran.
I got so tired of the way things were
I just started running.
"No one listens to me," I cried
    and I started running.
"I'm the only one around here who cares," I cried
    and I started running.
"If I stick around here I'll go crazy," I cried
    and I started running.

"No one understands me," I cried
    and I started running.

And I ran and I ran and I ran.
I ran for days
    and weeks
    and months
    and years.
I ran into new problems
    and I kept running.

And when I could run no longer
    I stopped.

I tried to catch my breath,
and then I yelled out loud,
    I said:
    "God!
    Listen to me.
    I want answers.
    I want some respect.
    I want some attention.
    I want…
    I want…
    I…
    I…"

And I sat down to wait for an answer.

And I waited.

I said, "Come on, God, I'm waiting.
    You owe me an explanation

and I want it now.
I haven't got all day, you know."

And I heard nothing.

I said, "God, don't you care?
Don't you care about me?"

and I heard nothing.

I said, "That's it, God.
I'm giving you one more chance.
You'd better give me some answers,
or else I'll…
or else I'll…"

And I heard nothing.

And I waited.

And I waited.

And the silence was deafening.

And then I heard laughter,
starting small
getting louder.

It was my own voice;
I was laughing at myself.

And then
in the midst of the laughter
and the silence

I heard a gentle voice
and the gentle voice said:
    "are you ready to listen?"
and then

I heard God speak.

Surprised by Healing

(Naaman)

Scripture reference: 2 Kings 5:1–14

How often do we judge places—and people and things for that matter—by their size? Anything of any worth or importance ought to look big and, well, important. Yet God is so often challenging this view. Worth and value are inherent in so many things, regardless of size, appearance, and reputation.

The huge limousine driving down the dusty, desert road seemed so hopelessly out of place, an affront to everything that one might consider normal. It drove past miles of nothingness, punctuated only by the occasional boulder, a tree or cactus seeming to gasp for water, or a rusting vehicle.

When the car pulled to a stop in front of the near-abandoned garage, all life seemed to stop for a moment. It seemed, in fact, that life often stopped here anyway, any chance it could get.

The man sitting outside the garage registered what passed for shock simply by making enough movement to suggest that he was, in fact, alive.

The limousine driver got out and opened the back door, and an impeccably dressed gentleman stepped gingerly out of the car.

"Can I help you?" asked the garage man, not bothering to stand up. "You seem like you might be lost." The huge overstatement of the obvious might have gotten a laugh or chuckle elsewhere, but it was simply too hot and isolated a place, and the people too different from each other, for them to share any kind of humor.

"I'm, uh, looking for Jordan's garage," the gentleman offered, surveying his surroundings.

"Stop looking. You've found it. Though I've gotta tell you, not a lot of folks ever look for us. They just kind of drive along and find us. Name's Jack. Fill 'er up?"

"Uh, yes, sure," the man said distractedly, "although that's not exactly why we're here." He kept looking around, nervously, as if he were expecting to see something that would put his mind at ease, but even he wasn't sure what.

"Well, we got one of the best mechanics you'll find anywhere. Getting parts for that thing might take a while, though. We don't get a whole o' limousines stopping by."

"I'm sure you don't," offered the driver. As Jack put the nozzle in the tank, the driver and the gentleman looked nervously at each other, questioning, wondering, not at all sure that this was the way things were supposed to go.

"We're looking for something."

"Well, I've been here all my life," Jack said. "If it's around here, I'm sure I can help you find it. What is it you're looking for?" He looked straight at the gentleman, who in turn deferred to the driver.

"As you can gather, we've come from away. My boss—Mr. Naaman—he, uh, he's not well. Tried every doctor we could find, here *and* overseas. Nothing seems to be working. He's tried all the alternative cures, everything. That's why we're here. He's so very desperate, you see. And a young girl—works for him, as a matter of fact, helps out around the house—comes from out this way, and she was adamant that someone here could help him out. Absolutely insisted that we come here."

"Here?" the man asked incredulously. He waited for the word to sink in and then asked it again. "Here?"

He began to laugh. "I think you took the wrong turn somewhere back along the way! Your car we can fix, but not your boss."

"I understand. But the girl was insistent. Jordan's Garage, route 7. There isn't another...?" he let the words trail off, knowing the answer already.

"Nope. This is it. But we're a garage, I'm afraid, not a hospital."

"Well, is there somewhere else nearby that she might have meant?" Mr. Naaman asked.

"Look for yourself," the man answered, sweeping his hand across the empty and pointless horizon.

"Hey, Jack," a voice called from under a vehicle at the back of the garage. "Send them back here."

"That's my mechanic, Eli," Jack explained to the strangers, almost apologetically. And then, turning towards the back, he called out "he's looking for a doctor, not a mechanic."

"I know. Send him back here."

The driver looked at Naaman, who looked back at the driver, his eyes searching for advice, for an answer, for a solution, for something, for anything.

"I know what he needs; send him back here," Eli called out once again.

"Well, you heard the man. Although I don't know what he knows that I don't" Jack shrugged.

A hush came over the trio standing outside. The driver indicated with a nod of his head that Naaman ought to at least check it out. Slowly, the gentleman turned and walked into the garage.

"You don't know how difficult this has been for him," the driver, whose name was David, said quietly to Jack. "No one will go near him at home. He can't go anywhere without people getting up and leaving the room the minute he walks in. All his money, and he just sits around, a prisoner in his own house. And he's such a caring man! Used to be involved in all sorts of volunteer work. You might not know it to look at him, but he used to go every week to the children's hospital and play guitar and sing with them. And he was always being invited for tennis, golf, you name it. That is, when he wasn't on the phone. People from all over the world used to call him—he was a consultant to some of the best.

"Now, since he got sick, people won't even talk to him. People that used to admire him say the worst things about him. His wife, she sticks by him, but the strain's been hard on her, too. Even the help quit; that's why they've got this young girl staying with them. Mr. Naaman had helped her out, and she said she'd come and stay with them, that she wasn't bothered by his, you know, condition. She's the one that told him about this place."

"You've stuck by him," Jack said.

"Well, I've got a brother who's got the same thing as him, you see, and so I guess I understand a little better than some. But, you know, it's been—" He was cut short by the hurried and angry return of Naaman from the garage.

"Of all the nerve!" he sputtered, as he motioned for the driver to open the car door.

"Is there a problem, boss?"

"Of all the nerve!" Naaman repeated. He sat down in disgust.

"Didn't go well, eh?"

"You know what that imbecile wanted? He wanted me to go and sit in some stupid little creek—naked, no less."

"And?" asked the driver.

"And, nothing. That's it. Just go down that ravine back there, take my clothes off, and sit in the middle of some piddly little creek for a while. And not only that, he didn't even bother to come out from under the car he was working on. Oh, of all the nerve…"

There was a pause while everyone collected their thoughts.

"Have you seen the size of that creek?" Naaman continued. "And God only knows what's in it. I could have sat in a zillion streams back home—ones with clear water, I might add. The gall of that man—why didn't he just say he couldn't help me? It's an insult."

"I kind of understand your frustration, boss," David said. "I mean, to come all of this way and everything." He paused for a long breath. "Perhaps you could just try it. I mean, what have you got to lose?"

"My dignity, that's what. I'd look like a fool. And if all I had to do was sit in three inches of water, I could have stayed home."

The driver took another long breath. "Boss, if he told you to dance on one leg with needles stuck in your arm and dead mouse on your head, you'd probably have done it, right?"

"Well, I don't know..."

"So the problem here is that it's just too simple?"

Naaman looked off a bit uncomfortably. "I suppose it is."

"Then why don't you try it? If it doesn't work, who's to know? *I'm* certainly not going to say anything." They both looked at Jack who immediately shook his head, as if on cue. "And, boss, you never know..."

"Oh all right," Naaman said. The tone of his voice almost sounded relieved, as if he'd been waiting for someone to give him permission.

"Do you want me to come with you and hold your clothes for you?"

"No," Naaman replied, "I think I'll do this on my own."

"Give a shout if you need me, then."

Naaman walked the path behind the garage. He looked back over his shoulder a couple of times, as if he were afraid that they were all having a good laugh as his expense. But Jack had gone back inside, and the driver just motioned him on.

When he was out of sight, David and Jack went inside, and shared a drink and a game of cards. They talked of vital things like football scores and weather, as one does in a garage.

A shout punctuated the oppressive heat.

"David!"

The driver looked up in panic.

"David! Come quickly!"

Dropping his cards, the driver dashed outside and around to the back, to see Naaman clambering over the rocks towards him, stark naked.

"David! I'm cured! I don't believe it, I'm cured!"

David stumbled down to meet him.

"I'm cured, David," Naaman repeated again as the two men met and embraced. "I don't know what it is about that water but, look, I'm my old self again."

"I can't believe it, Boss! It's fantastic." The two men jumped up and down, shouting like children. Any sense of distance embedded in the employer/employee relationship vanished, at least for the moment. Jack came out of the garage to see what was going on.

"I'm happy for you," Jack commented. "Now, I'd be putting some clothes on before you get a sunburn."

Naaman, until that moment oblivious to the fact that he was still naked, got dressed and the three of them walked back to the garage.

"I owe your mechanic my thanks, and an apology. I don't know what he did, but it worked."

They went inside, where Eli had just crawled out from underneath the vehicle on which he'd been working, and stood there wiping his hands on a rag.

"Thank you, thank, you, thank you," Naaman said. "I'm so sorry I underestimated you. That water has some pretty miraculous healing powers."

"It's not the water," Eli said quietly.

"Of course it is! Look, all my sores are gone. I'm like a new person!"

"Oh, there's no question that you're better," Eli replied. "But it's not the water that did it. It was God."

"Well, you must have a more powerful God than I have, because I've been praying for years and nothing's happened until now."

"God brings great healing," Eli said. "Tell me, what did you think about when you were sitting in the creek?"

"Well," Naaman looked about, a bit embarrassed, "mostly I thought what a fool I must look, sitting there naked as the day I was born, out here in the middle of nowhere. And then, I started thinking about the river I used to swim in when I was a boy, and of my childhood and…It's funny how your mind works, isn't it? I started remembering some of the things that I'd done in my life, and thanking God for places I'd been, and experiences I'd had. To be honest with you, I kind of forgot that I was sick and, when I looked down, I realized I was cured."

"Healed," Eli said. "You're healed, which is more than being cured. The sores may come back, you know, and you'll have days when your body just won't do what you want it to do."

"But I feel great!" Naaman countered.

"I believe you," Eli went on. "You're healed. It's not quite the same; it's stronger. It lasts longer. Being healed is knowing that God is with you, knowing that you are still a person of worth, knowing that you can do things, and be someone. I don't want you to be discouraged when you have bad days, and think that the water failed you. It wasn't the water. It was taking the time to focus not on your pain, but on God's presence. As long as you can do that, you will be healed."

"But I don't understand. Why would God do this now, when I've been praying for so long? Is it that I didn't pray the right way? Did I not use the right words? Was I not good enough? What?"

"I don't think it's any of that," Eli said. "I think it's that you were too scared before. I think when you let go of some of your fear, God was able to enter in. You let your guard down, and made an opening for God."

"Well, whatever it is, I'm grateful. So very grateful." Naaman turned to the driver. "Let's go, David. I can't wait to get home and tell everyone."

"Don't forget what happened here," Eli said.

"Oh, I won't," Naaman replied assuredly.

"No, I mean don't forget what *really* happened here. When things get difficult or painful again, don't forget that it was your fear that was the problem. Your fear made you put up walls to keep God out. Remember that, and trust. God will be there."

There were handshakes all around, and Naaman and David got into the limousine and turned down the road.

As they drove away, Jack and Eli went back into the garage.

"Did you get that job finished?" Jack asked.

"Almost," Eli replied. "Just have to change the oil. I'll get right to it."

"You do that," Jack said.

Talking with Mother

Scripture reference: Hosea 11:1–11

I don't want to give this one an introduction, but just let it stand on its own.

She walked slowly across the studio floor: frail, to be sure, yet so certain of every step. Her brown face glowed with a satisfied air, almost playful, unquestionably loving, strong, and gentle.

She sat on the couch that immediately tried to dwarf her, as if anything, or anyone, could diminish the strength that shone from her very being.

The television host acknowledged her with a smile and a nod, and then turned to face the cameras.

"Our program tonight is on mothers, and with me in the studio is a woman who has been a mother for a long time."

She smiled. "That's certainly true."

"So tell me: any regrets?"

"Oh no, not at all. At least, not in the long term. There are certainly times when I've thought, 'what's the point?' But those moments always go quickly."

"Why so many children?"

"It's my nature; I can't help it."

"Before our audience gets the wrong impression here, I should say that they're all adopted, is that correct?"

"That's right. And I love them all—can't help but love them all. They *need* so much, you know? It doesn't matter how grown up they get, they still need me. And, I suppose, in a way, I need them. I need to love—it's all I know. Sometimes, it's 'tough love' as they say, but it's always love."

"What about when they disobey you?"

"That's when they need love the most. It's a funny thing: they do something really horrible, call you all sorts of names, and then run away and…you want them back. You don't want them to do it again, but you want them back. And you know that you'll welcome them back, even go and chase them down sometimes, and you'll scold them and lecture them, and hug them and bathe them in tears. And, you know that, in one form or another, they'll go right back out and do it again, and you'll love them all over again."

"One might think you're a doormat…"

"I don't think so. A doormat never reacts or responds, does it? I do. I let them know my feelings. A doormat just sits there, uncaring. But I care. I tell them when I'm hurting. I tell them they've *done* the hurting, and what it feels like. They've sat in the corner more than once, too, I can tell you that! But you *have* to love them. You have to; there's no two ways about it."

"Your children have sometimes said some pretty nasty things about you."

"They have. Some of them like to deny that I'm even their mother. I can understand that—it's all part of growing up, you know, needing to establish their identity, that sort of thing. The ones that really hurt are the ones who say they love me, and then go on to describe me in ways that make my skin crawl. Saying that I play favorites, that I have a pecking order at my table. It's all a load of malarkey!"

"So they might not be welcome at your table any more themselves, is that it?"

"Of course they're welcome! They're always welcome at my table, and they can call on me whenever they want—even reverse the charges if they have to—but I'll want them to explain themselves when they get here, you can be sure of that. We'll have a long talk. And it may not be too comfortable for them. Ask them some time about one of our 'talks' and they'll tell you that I do most of the talking, and they do the listening! Even when they try and fill the air with words, somehow I manage to get my point across. I have my ways!" She chuckled with an impish little smile.

"So how do you do it? Don't you get tired?"

"Yes."

"Have you ever thought of packing it all in? Retiring?"

"There are days when the thought has crossed my mind. But I wouldn't know how. It wouldn't be me. How do you retire from being a parent? How do you retire from loving? If you love, it's unconditional—there are no strings, no expiry dates, no clauses that let you off the hook. It goes on forever. I know no other kind. It's who I am. I am what I am. It's that simple."

Star Followers

(The Magi)

Scripture reference: Matthew 2:1–12

Matthew tells us precious little about the magi; legends, hymns, and traditions tell us far more. How many were there? Men or women? The Bible is silent. So, I imagined a couple. And instead of camels, I went all out and gave them a car...

The inquisitive eyes took it all in: the fancy car, the foreign license plates. She hadn't read anything on the roster about any kind of state visit—who were these people? A man and a woman, definitely with money, and definitely not from around here. And just showing up like that!

People don't simply drive up to a royal palace, all nonchalant-like, and expect to get admitted. The tourists who got to see the formal sitting room and the office, they got their tickets well in advance and stood in a line out back for hours. But these two drove up and marched right up to the front door. This, Abigail decided, needed some investigation. Didn't people know that nothing was really supposed to happen around here without her approval? She might be the maid, but everyone knew that in reality she ran the place. Even visitors were supposed to instinctively know that. I mean, really.

What's more, Abigail saw Reuben, the security guard at the front door, let them in, as if he'd been expecting them.

"Oh, I hope they come to my wing," she thought as she let the curtain drop back into place. "I'd better go and see what's going on."

She rushed down the hallway, and was in luck.

"Abigail, these are the Kashmalis, guests from Persia," the security guard said. "They've just arrived, and will be staying with us for a few days. Would you show them to the suite overlooking the south garden?"

"Certainly, Reuben," she replied, trying to sound appropriate and not overcome with glee. Now she had a chance to find out what the real story was. "Please come with me," she added, almost as an afterthought.

"So, you're from Persia," Abigail said, as they began to make their way down the long corridor. "How lovely. I've not been there myself, but I hear it's very nice. Kashmali…that's a pretty important name, isn't it?"

"Well, I suppose so," said the woman. "We don't like to make much of it—my husband's family is in the oil business, and his sister's in the government. But please, you can call us Petra and Alex."

"Oh, that wouldn't do. I'm very proper, I am. Trained to be." A slight pause. "Oh, all right, if you insist. My name's Abigail." She offered them a big smile by way of formal greeting. "So, had a long journey, then?" Abigail continued, as they came to the end of the corridor and started up the staircase.

"I should say so," Alex answered. "We've been on the road for months."

"Really? You've not come direct on the new highway, then?" Abigail immediately felt a little silly—the answer was obviously "no."

"No." He might have said more, but a furtive glance from Petra caused his words to trail off.

"Well, you'll be glad of a chance to rest. Here we are." She flung open the door to the suite with great flourish. "You make yourselves at home, I'll draw you nice hot baths."

"That would be lovely."

As she went into the adjoining bathroom, Abigail said to herself, "All right, there's definitely something peculiar here. But how to find out without appearing too nosy, that's the rule of the game, Abigail dear."

While the guests took their baths, Abigail busied herself with small tasks in the room, setting out their things, fluffing the pillows until they were beyond fluffing, adjusting the windows for the umpteenth time.

"I picked up this paper that fell out of your briefcase," she said to Alex. "Put it there on the night stand. Some kind of map, is it?" Abigail had never been very good at subtlety when fishing for information.

"It's a star chart, actually," he said, offering to show it to her.

"Ooh, I don't know a thing about that sort of thing," Abigail replied.

"It's quite fascinating. Here, let me show you." The two of them leaned over the chart. "This is what you see on a clear night, all of the stars lighting up the Persian sky. This is the reason it took us so long to get here—we've been using this as our map."

"Well no wonder! Me, I don't travel much, but whenever I do, I take a map that shows the roads on the ground. You mark my words, it's much easier to follow!"

"That it would be. But you see, we've been following a particular star. It's a rare phenomenon, a moving star. Brighter than anything in all the heavens. That's what led us here, actually."

"What?" Abigail asked. "We've got a big star overhead, do we?"

"Well, as a matter of fact, no," Alex sighed. "The thing is, we've sort of lost it. But we know that King Herod has astrologers on staff, so we've come here in hopes of gaining a little of their expertise."

"It's all beyond me. I don't go up to the observatory, I'm strictly a guest room maid. But I hear they've got all the latest equipment up there—telescopes, computers, you name it. If you've lost a star, I'm sure they can find it for you."

"To tell you the truth," Petra said, "it's not the star we're looking for. It's what the star is pointing to that we're really interested in."

"Now that sounds mysterious. Some sort of pot of gold at the end of the rainbow, is it?"

"Better than that. A person. An important person."

"What sort of person?" Abigail asked.

"Well, that's just it," Alex said. "We don't really know. All we know is that, whenever one of these types of stars appears, the world is in for mystical and wonderful changes. And as we've wondered and talked and dreamed about this star—and with what we've read in the scientific journals and such—we're convinced that it signifies some new kind of leader."

"And so we've been searching," Petra continued. "We've been studying the stars for years now, and we believe that one has led us near here. We've pored over the writing from this area, and believe it has to do with the birth of a unique and divine leader. But we're still not exactly sure who we're looking for."

Abigail's face lit up.

"I know who you're looking for."

"You do?" Alexa and Petra both stared at her in disbelief.

"Yes. You're looking for the Messiah. Join the club—the people of Israel have been waiting for centuries for the Messiah. God's chosen one, going to come and rule in justice and peace. A proper leader, a servant king. One who turns the world upside down and right side up again."

"A new king?" Alex said excitedly. "Then we *are* in the right place. Surely King Herod must know all about this!"

Abigail was quiet for a moment. "If you don't mind my saying so, sir, I don't think you quite understand." She looked worriedly around the room, and then lowered her voice. "It's more than my job's worth—probably more than my life's worth, if the truth be known—but you seem like good people, so let me tell you something you ought to know.

"The Messiah's going to be a different kind of king, not like this one we've got now. He's no king—he's a ruthless, money-grubbing playboy if you want to know the half of it. Couldn't care less about anyone except himself. Has no time for God. Treats people like things. Treats a stray dog better than members of his own family some times. And let's face it, most kings are all the same. Power—it goes to their heads. But the Messiah…the Messiah will be different. The Messiah will rule with justice, in God's way. Bring down the mighty, lift up the lowly, level out the playing field. Share things around, balance things out. A whole new world."

Abigail was interrupted by a knock on the door. The guests were being summoned for a meeting with the king.

"I may be just a simple house maid," Abigail whispered as they were leaving, "but if you want my advice, I'd urge you not to tell him any more than you have to. Fish for information, but don't give him much. You never know just what he'll do with it. But mind, *I* didn't tell you that."

Some time later, Alex and Petra returned to their room. Abigail, who had been watching and waiting for them, soon knocked on the door, ostensibly bringing tea, but really just to ask questions.

"Please, yes, come in," Petra said.

"Well, how was his majesty today?" Abigail asked.

"Oh, very shocked and curious about our quest," Alex answered.

"Let me guess, tried to act nonchalant and polite, didn't he, and acted as if everything were under control?"

"Why, yes."

"And urged you to let him know how you make out, didn't he?"

"Yes."

"Don't be fooled. He's a sneaky so and so. He doesn't care about you or anybody else, only himself. Did he tell you where you ought to go?"

"Well, no," Petra said, "but we're going to meet with some of the astrologers after dinner, and they're going to help us. It can't be far."

"I'll tell you then, shall I?"

"What?" They both expressed surprise. "You know where to find the Messiah? How?"

"It's not far, and yet I suppose it might as well be. My grandmother used to tell us stories about the Messiah. She didn't know when he would come, but she told us the scriptures were clear about where he'd be born. Just a few miles down the road, in Bethlehem."

"Bethlehem?"

"Yes. It was the city of King David. And our people have known for years that that's where the Messiah will be born. Only Herod, he's so smart, he doesn't know anything."

"But Bethlehem's such a backwards little place," Alex ventured.

"Exactly," Abigail said. "And when you get there, look for the Messiah in the most unexpected place, and you'll find him. When you look for God in familiar, traditional ways, you can get disappointed. When you think you know where God is, when you think you have God figured out, well, things tend not to go the way you'd planned. But when you are open to different possibilities, somehow, God's right there."

"It doesn't make sense," Petra said.

"But does it have to?" Alex asked. "After all, this whole journey doesn't really make sense, and yet somehow it seems right."

"Go to Bethlehem," Abigail urged. "Follow your hearts. If the Messiah is there, God will lead you to him. But I'd go quickly if I were you. And I wouldn't let King Herod know."

"He's offered to send some guides with us," Alex said, "to help us in our search."

"You mark my words, they want to find him for only one thing—to kill him. No, you must go alone, and quickly. And when you find the child, warn his family to get him to safety. We must not let God's chosen one be overcome by the likes of Herod."

"Abigail, you've been so good to help us," Petra said. "Alex, I think she's right—we should leave now."

"You're right. You've been wonderful, Abigail. Thank you."

"I'm only glad I could help. May God watch over you in your search."

"Thank you," Petra said. "We'll write to you and let you know how everything works out."

"Oh, you needn't do that," Abigail smiled. "I'll know."

She watched them leave and closed the door behind them.

"I'll know."

Magnificat

Scripture reference: Luke 1:26–56

One day at Bible class we were discussing the Magnificat and someone asked, "Who wrote it down?" Well, the scholar in me wanted to say something like "Luke wrote it down. It might be based on something Mary said, but Luke wrote it." But then the dreamer in me started wondering how it might have come to pass, and I imagined Elizabeth greeting Zechariah when he came home from Temple duty that evening.

Oh Zechariah, I'm so glad to see you. How was your day? Oh that's right, I'm sorry: you can't talk. Well, let me tell you about my day.

Mary's here—Anna's girl—she's lying down in the spare room right now.

37

Zechariah, she's pregnant. I know, only fourteen years old, and not married, but these things happen. And Zechariah, she should be scared stiff, but she's not!

I mean, here I am with a loving husband to care for me, and I've thought and dreamed for years about having a baby, and I've attended many a birth in my time—I know what I'm in for, and still I'm half scared out of my mind. But not Mary! Something's come over that girl; it's amazing.

She arrived on the doorstep and, you know, it's as if I knew she was coming. What's more—now I know you're going to think I'm a crazy old woman, Zechariah, and maybe I am—but I'd swear our baby knew she was coming, too.

I was standing at the table kneading bread dough when I felt the baby leap inside me. I know he's kicked before—he's a feisty little character—but today was different. When I felt it, I just knew something special was going to happen. And I looked up, and there was Mary.

Oh, Zechariah, she was glowing! I knew she was expecting—she doesn't show or anything, but I could just tell.

Well, I was worried. They haven't gotten married yet, and you know how people talk. But Mary, she didn't have a worry in the world.

She was just bursting with incredible news: about an angel, about the Messiah, about God's love for all people. And about how lucky she was. Imagine that Zechariah, thinking about all of that at her age.

We sat out in the garden drinking lemonade, and we talked about babies, and life, and dreams, and stories.

"I feel just like Hannah, the prophet Samuel's mother," she said.

I laughed. "If anyone feels like Hannah, it should be me. Pregnant at my age, after all these years. Hannah was quite past her prime, too, when Samuel was born."

"That's true," Mary said, "and your baby is going to be special, Elizabeth. I just know that something incredible is about to happen. God has not been absent, all these years. God has been quietly preparing."

"Preparing for what?" I asked.

"To do something new. You know all the promises God has made to us, ever since the time of Abraham and Sarah? I think God is fulfilling those promises now, through us—through our babies."

She began to move about the garden in a slow and spirited kind of dance, moving and swaying as she spoke.

"God is doing something amazing, Elizabeth. In fact, it's already begun, I just know it. Some might look on me as a nobody, as an insignificant young girl from the backstreets of nowhere, and yet God is changing the world through me—through *us*. I'm not just having any baby, Elizabeth, I'm carrying the Messiah! And your child will be a prophet. I suppose in a way, that makes us prophets, too.

"You see, God is tired of injustice and will stand for it no longer. The rich and powerful have had their day; they are finished. But the poor, the meek, the hungry, the downtrodden, the lonely, the hurting: God will bless them. They will have new life. Those whom others have looked down on for so long will find themselves standing tall and proud."

I wish I could tell you how enthusiastic she was, Zechariah, but it isn't possible to capture. She was just so alive. I felt God's spirit in the air.

Something is going on, Zechariah, I can feel it. I *know* it. I'm not sure exactly how it will all unfold, but I know that God has some amazing things in store. And you and me and our baby, and Mary and her baby—we're all a part of it somehow.

You sense it too, don't you? I know you do. I wish you could tell me what you're thinking and feeling.

Oh, there—the baby's kicking again. Put your hand on my tummy. There—did you feel it?

Life is pretty incredible sometimes, isn't it Zechariah? What? Is that a tear? You don't have to hide it. It's okay to cry.

A Child Is Born

Scripture reference: Luke 2:1–20

We hear the word "inn" and imagine a hotel with a tired, frustrated desk clerk who turns away a couple of poor people in the middle of the night because the place is overbooked. But maybe that's not quite it. Hotel? The New Jerusalem Bible *more accurately translates it as "living-space." Probably Mary and Joseph would have sought out relatives.*

The story changes a little if I recognize that it was undoubtedly a family member—albeit a distant one—who rejected Mary and Joseph that night. The stable, too, was hardly the pretty little barn that we see in our Christmas nativity scenes. Rather it was more likely a cave or shed in which animals, and "lower-class" people, stayed together. The shepherds and goatherds and their families probably stayed with the animals in the back of the house. It wasn't the most ideal place to have a baby perhaps, but a place full of love and warmth just the same.

She was scared.

Scared and tired.

Scared and tired and angry.

"How could they make us travel all this distance?" she wondered.

Mary shifted for the umpteenth time, and realized yet again that she would not be comfortable, that's all there was to it.

She looked at Joseph. Weary as she was, she still could take some comfort in the image of the strong, sturdy man walking beside her.

Mary adored him with all her heart. She had always admired him and, when she learned they were to be married, she was overjoyed. But fear had swept over her when she learned she was pregnant. Would he believe her incredible story? Why should he?

He had stormed from her house in disgust and anger, leaving her so alone, so terrified, so much as if she were dead, even with the new life inside her. How amazed she had been when he returned to her home and spoke not to her but to her parents.

"She is with child," Joseph said, "and I am the father. Might we move up the date of the wedding feast, and live together sooner as man and wife?"

As she listened to him speak that falsehood in order to spare her life, Mary knew then that he loved her, that he was a man of compassion and gentleness. No other man she knew would have done that, would have risked the public shame that Joseph was facing. Most would have left her to fend for herself, which was no option for a pregnant girl in that world.

And he treated her so well! Sometimes he'd gently place his hand on her belly, not speaking, just smiling. Approaching the strange village and all the uncertainty that lay ahead, she needed this memory.

"How will we know where to go?" she asked again.

"My people are the sheep owners in this town. My father says that they have always lived on the hillside. We'll go to the first house there, and explain who we are. They're bound to give us a room for the night. We're family; it's an obligation."

"But what if they don't believe you?" Mary asked worriedly.

"They have to believe me. They know that so many people are on the move. They'll believe me." His voice was not as sure as his words, and the two of them continued on in silence, moving among the crowds and confusion. They arrived at the first house leaning hard into the hill.

Joseph went to the door; Mary watched in anxious silence. "He's taking too long," she thought. She was scared.

"I tried to explain," Joseph began when he returned to her, "and they were sympathetic. But they just don't have the room. So many other family members have already arrived. They were most apologetic."

"But what are we going to do?" she asked in desperation. "Where else can we go?"

"Well, they said we could stay with the hired folk out with the animals. It's warm, and out of the wind. And it will be a lot quieter than in the house, actually. We'll be able to get a good night's sleep."

"Is it far?"

"No, it's just there, behind the house, that sort of cave. There's a fire." And with that they took the final few steps.

An older woman greeted them with suspicion.

"Who sent you?" she asked.

"The master of the house said that we could stay the night here," Joseph answered. "We're family, from Nazareth."

The woman looked past Joseph to Mary, and her face softened.

"You'd better get in out of the cold. My name is Judith. This is my husband Yitzhak. Come and rest here on the straw."

As they settled in, Mary realized that the place *was* warm, and the faces gentle, and it wasn't quite so bad after all. Children, donkeys, chickens, and a nanny goat watched the couple inquisitively.

"Your time is not far off," Judith said, handing Mary a bowl of stew. "Your first?"

"Yes," Mary said.

"I was scared for my first, but it wasn't that bad, really. And I've gotten used to it now—seven times I've been blessed."

"Seven!?" Mary said with alarm.

"There's no law says you have to follow in my footsteps, child!" Judith laughed. And Joseph laughed. And Mary laughed. And the others laughed.

There was a lot of love in the stable, and much storytelling about birth and life and hope and joy. For the first time in days, Mary relaxed a little, and felt safe. And it was only as she was falling off to sleep, nestled in Joseph's arms, that she felt the first sharp pain.

Joseph snapped to alertness when he heard Mary cry. Judith reached for a lamp with one hand and felt Mary's belly with the other.

"It will be soon," she said and began the preparations.

Joseph held Mary's hand through the pain, and Judith encouraged her through it all, and the night moved on, and the child was born, and there was love, and there was warmth, and there was welcome.

As morning began to dawn, others came in from the fields, and as they stared at the mother and child their tiredness melted away. They talked about feeling God's presence all around them in that place, and how it filled them over-brimming with joy and hope. They ran out and told others of the child born that night amongst the animals.

Mary would always remember the light—the warmth of the fire reflected in Judith's eyes as she had helped her, and the radiance of her new-born child, and how the stars seemed brighter that night than any other before or since.

John the Baptist and the Brood of Vipers

Scripture reference: Luke 3:1–18; Matthew 3:1–12

I had always assumed that John was angry when he saw the religious leaders coming to hear him. But maybe his response was different, and so in this treatment of the story I tried to offer an altered tone of voice—a touch of sarcasm, perhaps...

"Well, well, well. What have we here?"

John had no sooner sat down to take a drink of water than one of his disciples pointed out a rather well-dressed crowd coming over the hill from town.

"Decided it was time to listen to the prophets did you?"

John took a sip of water but, just as one of the visitors began to speak, John raised up his hand to stop them.

"Now, now, before you say anything, I've heard it all. You think you know all the ins and outs of serving God because you've been born into the faith: you've heard it from the day you were born, memorized Bible verses 'til you were blue in the face, given appropriate offerings at the appropriate times, and even gone to worship on regular occasions—barely missed a holiday, have you?" He let them feel guilty for a brief moment, then let them see him smile. "It's okay. God can just as quickly raise up a congregation of these stones as gather in you lot.

"No, my friends…" John stood up. "God's looking for a little more than just a bunch of deadwood. God wants some living trees that can bear good fruit. God knows that you can recite the prophets' words, but can you live them? That's what God wants to know."

"What kinds of things do we have to do?" they asked, showing genuine interest.

"It's simple, really," John replied. "You, over there, when you go to harvest? Share it with those who have no food. You with the extra coat, give one away.

"You tax collectors," (there was an audible grumbling in the crowd), "it's all right that you do that for a living, but be fair about it. That goes for anyone in business. Same thing for you soldiers—don't go bullying and throwing your weight around.

"It's the basics that God has been talking about for ages. Love, not animal sacrifice. Justice, kindness. Living God's simple truths day to day. That's why I offer this water—a chance to wash clean and start over.

"But there's an even more wonderful new beginning yet to come. God is sending someone who offers new life in ways you cannot even begin to imagine. The One who is to come will bring God's Spirit to cleanse and renew you like never before—a fire to burn away all of the useless, worthless parts of your lives, and to strengthen you and prepare you for God's service in wonderful ways.

"So, who wants to be in on this one?"

That Preacher

(John the Baptist)

Scripture reference: Luke 3:1–18; Matthew 3:1–12

Too often, I think we hear the call to repentance as judgment, rather than the opportunity for a new beginning that it represents. John the Baptist invited people to something quite wonderful—a chance to start over.

It wasn't my idea to go, you see. It was the wife's.

"You should go and hear him," she said. "It's Betty and Zack's boy, preaching down by the river. He says some good stuff, I think you'd like what he has to say. Besides, it'll do you good to get out of the house."

I didn't want to argue so I went.

I want to be clear, though, I'm not big on preachers. Too much fluffy, pie in the sky nonsense as far as I'm concerned. But I hadn't seen young

John since he was a boy, and I was curious. Thought I'd stop for five minutes on the way back from the market.

I must say, John had drawn quite a crowd! He stood on an outcropping of rock, looking like he'd spent a little too long in the hot sun.

Seems he was addressing some religious leaders—loudly.

"Don't think for one second," John said, "that you can rest on your laurels just because you think you're God's chosen ones. Oh no; you have to turn your lives around. Completely around.

"God is concerned with righteous behavior, not in who you know, or in who you think you are."

He looked around. "Why, God could find more righteousness in these rocks right here than in a lot of you!"

I laughed along with the rest of the crowd; this John was all right! I'd always thought some of the religious leaders needed to be brought down a peg or two.

"You need to offer your whole self to God," he continued.

An elderly couple stepped forward. "But how do we do that?" the woman asked.

"By doing what God wants," John replied. "By living the way the scriptures tell you. By seeking justice, loving, kindness, walking humbly with God."

"But what does that really *mean?*" asked the man. He sounded a little frustrated.

John looked straight at them—kindly, mind you, not harshly. "Share your lunch with your neighbor. Offer someone who's homeless a bed for the night."

The couple sat down quickly, and a tax collector stood up. "What should someone like me do?" he asked.

"Don't collect more than your fair share. No more skimming profits off the top."

Well, everyone started talking at once. It sounded like a hive of bees had been suddenly let loose. But when four huge Roman soldiers approached, the air fell silent as a tomb.

"What about us?" one of them asked. "Do you have any advice for us?"

We'd all seen soldiers slice people's heads off for sport; were they setting John a trap?

He faced them squarely. "Don't take advantage of your uniform and your authority. Don't go into people's homes and steal, just because you've got all the might of Rome on your side. Don't accuse people of crimes they haven't committed. Don't take advantage of the women here. Just because you've been sent somewhere you don't want to be, don't take it out on us; it's not our fault."

"You mean there's hope for us?" the shortest giant asked.

"There's hope for everyone," John said. "When the Messiah comes, he will offer salvation and new life to all."

John bent down and scooped up a handful of water and let it drip from his fingers. "I baptize you with water. But water only washes the surface. The Messiah will baptize with the Holy Spirit. You will be cleansed from the inside out.

"The Messiah will sift through every aspect of your life, like someone winnowing grain. The parts of your life that can bear good fruit will remain, but the chaff, all the things that are useless and weighing you down, the things that keep you from being God's people—all that will be blown away."

As if on cue, the wind blew a little, emphasizing John's words.

It was getting late. I had to get to market.

But I couldn't shake John's message as I went. Imagine, a chance to start over again.

I've thought many times since about John's advice to the different groups of people, about how they could live in keeping with God's will.

I've often wondered: what would he have said to me, if I had dared to ask?

Dear Jesus

(Temptations in the Wilderness)

Scripture reference: Matthew 4:1–11; Luke 4:1–13;

While somewhat tongue in cheek—perhaps even irreverent—this is my attempt to understand the temptations that Jesus faced in terms of my own life, rather than as something spiritual and, thus, potentially removed from the nitty gritty of everyday living.

Dear Jesus:

I've been wondering for quite some time now about those temptations everyone always talks about, and have a few questions, if I might be so bold.

You see, the thing that's been bothering me is that there were just the two of you out there in the wilderness (well, until those angels showed up) and so either you or the tempter had to report the story and, seeing as he doesn't come off very well in the whole thing I'm guessing it was you that told it and, well, you being such a modest sort and all, I can't really see you sitting around the campfire with the disciples saying, "here's a story that tells how great I am." Just doesn't fit my image of you somehow. So I began to think if just maybe there might be more to it, Jesus, and wondered if you could tell me. This is what I've come up with so far:

Okay, the stones and bread thing—I've never been that hungry, to be honest. I mean, I've had some times when I've said "I'm starving" but on the grand scale of human existence, it doesn't really count. So I wondered if maybe it wasn't so much about food as it was about trying to take the easy way out. Because I *have* had those times when I've quickly glanced over my shoulder to see if anyone was looking, and thought I could get away with something.

Like the other day when I thought it would have been so much easier to throw out that big toner cartridge from the computer printer, rather than take it back to the office supply store so they could recycle it. I know those things are a terrible environmental hazard but come on, what's one lousy cartridge? Then I thought for a moment: that's the point, isn't it? What *is* one? It's a part of the whole, of the big picture. *I* am a part of the big picture. I can't take the easy way out. I have a part to play, a role, a responsibility, however insignificant it might seem at the moment. If I keep taking the easy way out, it sort of adds up, doesn't it? Is that the kind of temptation you were talking about?

I *do* think I can relate to number two, for sure. I've often looked out on my world—just listen to me, "my world"—and thought, "look at me. Look at what I've got. Look at how important I am." I can put myself on some pretty high and grand places, and think, "I've got it made. I've done it. I'm pretty darned special." Good Lord, Jesus, you know me: I've got an ego the size of Texas, and more besides. I've got a whole closet full of those "It's all about me" T-shirts.

I know only too well that so-called "devil worship" doesn't have anything to do with lighting candles at midnight or whatever—it has to do with me thinking I'm God, and wanting everyone else to treat me the same way. It's scary. It's dangerous. And sadly I do it more times than I care to mention.

I will say that I've never been tempted to try jumping off a tall building to see if God would catch me. It would be real easy to read those temptations and say, "hey, those don't apply to me." But that would take me right back to #2, above, wouldn't it. Because I have tried to put God to the test approximately 418,927.36 times. Approximately. Give or take.

They started out small, the things like "if you get me a new bike I'll read the Bible every day" and then escalated to "I really want you to change so-and-so's mind because they bug me and I know I'm right and I don't want to have to try to get along with them, I just want them to change so that the world will be a better place because, well, I want more people to be like me and if you do that, God, well, then I'll love and trust you just a little more." If I'm going to be honest, I have to put that in the "foolish test" column, don't I?

So anyway, Jesus, I don't want to take up more of your time, but I did want to check and see if I was on the right track. Please respond at your convenience. Although if you could answer directly, I'd appreciate it. Sometimes when Paul writes, I have trouble figuring out what he means.

Yours sincerely,
Donald

Herod's Letter

Scripture reference: Matthew 14:1–12; Mark 6:14–29

I find in the encounter of King Herod and John the Baptist a cloud of tragedy that extends beyond the assassination of John. While I cannot find any excuse for what Herod did, I cannot completely write Herod off as a despicable villain, rotten to the core. Instead, I find in his actions a bit of a parable—a sense of "there but for the grace of God go I." Because in this story I see yet another example of a person eaten up by ego, greed, and power—and in that, I think we're all at risk.

The story, as given to us by both Matthew and Mark, suggests that Herod felt trapped by his own words. I wonder, frankly, why he hadn't had John killed before, after some sham trial on grounds of treason. Perhaps Herod was intrigued by John, and haunted by him after death. And so, I imagined a letter that a broken Herod might have penned to the man he murdered in a moment of weakness.

Dear John:

I don't know why I'm writing this really. You'll never read it. You can't read it. You're dead. I killed you.

Oh God, do you know how that haunts me? Do you know how I wish I could go back and change things? I'd give anything for it to have turned out differently, John, you must believe me.

I thought myself a king, ruler of all I surveyed. But I'm not. I'm nothing, just a foolish old man, destined to travel the path of the living dead. What will become of me? Do you care? Strangely, even in death, I have the feeling that you do.

I wish I had had the courage to tell you, while you were alive, that you were right. But I couldn't bring myself to do it. Those nights when I would stagger down to your grimy cell, half drunk, relaxed enough to want to hear what you had to say.

You got to me. In my heart of hearts, I knew I had no right to be king. And no right to my beloved Herodias, either, even though I loved her. And it plagued me. Oh God, how it plagued me.

I was out of control, John. Caught up in the deceit of my stolen throne, the mirage of being king of the Jews, the intoxication of power and prestige. And the women. And the wine. And the wealth. I had it all.

Yet I had nothing.

My life was so hollow, so vacant, every crevice filled with fear and mistrust. And you knew that. All those times when I would hear you ranting and raving, I wanted to throttle you then, not because you were wrong, but because you were right. We both knew the truth, but I was too scared to admit it.

And then that night, that horrible, tragic night that sealed both our fates.

Caught up in a moment of heated lust, caught up in my own self-adoration, caught up in a promise I knew I had to keep just to save my own reputation. What did it gain me? Where has it left me?

I'm sure you understand Herodias' concern: if all your talk about our marriage being illegitimate had really taken hold, she would have been stoned to death, or tossed out in the streets to forage in the gutter like some discarded animal, and I couldn't do that to her, John. I love her, right or wrong. You must understand that.

Yet you know that I'm simply trying to justify it all, don't you? I could have found a way to keep her, to care for her. I could have sent her away to a secret place. I could have given up my throne. I could have done a thousand things, John, but I didn't. I let my greed and lust for power choke out every ounce of decency in my being. And now I have to live with that.

I'm sorry.

I know it can't possibly help you for me to say that, but somehow it helps me.

Though you cannot read this letter, perhaps you can at least hear my cries, and hear me begging God for forgiveness. And perhaps you, on behalf of the ages, might find that you can forgive me, too.

sincerely,
Herod of Galilee

The Prodigal, part 1

Scripture reference: Luke 15:11b–32

An aspect of this story that has always intrigued me is that the father ran towards his son. For a man to be able to run in those days, he had to hike up his long robes and expose his legs, and this was simply not done—it would be like someone today running down the street in their underwear. So great was the parent's enthusiasm to embrace the lost child that custom, protocol, and appearances became irrelevant. That is how eager God is to welcome us, Jesus says.

God is not just willing to receive us when we repent, but indeed is overwhelmed with an enthusiastic joy about it.

I do some of my best thinking when I'm shaving. It's a quiet, peaceful time, and I'm all alone. I like that.

The bathroom mirror affords a wonderful reflection through the top of the window, and I can see the road stretching off into infinity.

Ah, that road.

Sometimes I'll see a car or two driving by. Maybe an early morning bird checking out last night's road kill. If I'm running late, I notice the local kids heading out to the school bus.

I think of the times I have traveled down that road—a short jaunt to town, or the beginning of a journey to places far and beyond. And, of course, I think of coming down that road in the other direction, tired in the evening, and glad to be coming home.

It's down that road that my son left.

So many times I had watched him and his brother walking with their friends, headed for school. Or maybe riding their bikes, laughing and claiming ownership of the whole world.

But one day, my son went down that road, and didn't come back.

"Dad," he said, coming up to me when I was reading the paper, trying for all the world to act as if he was self-confident, but with every word almost quivering. "I was wondering, um, you know, um, you said that everything you owned would go to my brother and me when you and Mom died? Well, I was, um, just thinking that, um, well, my brother likes the farm and seems bent on sticking around here, so, why don't you give him the farm? I mean, I don't want it. Then you could, um, give me that money you've got saved in the bank, and we'd call it a deal? What do you say, Dad?"

He paused for a short second but, before I had a chance to say anything, continued quietly, "And, well, maybe I could have it, now? What do you think?"

Did it matter what I thought? We both knew what I would do. We both knew what he would do. Why argue with fate?

The day I handed him the cashier's check, we knew what was next, although we both clung briefly to a bit of denial.

"I think I'll maybe spend a bit of this, do some traveling. But I'll save the rest for college. I'm just going to take a few months to find myself, and then I'll go back to school in the Fall." Then he left the next morning, without saying goodbye.

We heard from him once, a postcard in January from Florida. That was it.

Three years went by. We wondered and worried. Each story of a hurricane, a riot, a bitter cold snap, unemployment, drug wars—they all made us look at each other a little more fearfully, and wonder, but we didn't talk about him. It seemed that words might somehow seal his uncertain fate.

The farm continued. We continued. But we ached.

How we ached.

Each morning, while I was shaving, I would notice that road. I thought at one point of even boarding up the window, so I wouldn't have to look. Tried drawing the shades a few times, but it felt wrong somehow. I needed to wonder. And after a while, it got easier to look at the road. But the pain never went away. Where was he?

One March morning, as a particularly cold winter was fighting to hang on against the inevitability of spring, I saw the road in the mirror. I stood, as usual, in my underwear and lathered up my face. I looked down as I rinsed the razor and, when I looked up, I saw a distant figure on the road. I couldn't identify it, but I didn't need to. I knew who it was.

I dropped the razor, dabbed at the cream on my face, and ran out of the bathroom. Taking the stairs two at a time (and thinking for a fractured second of the zillion times I had told the boys never to do that—funny the things you think of at the strangest times) I leapt out the door and ran up the road.

He stopped as I got closer, as if he didn't know what I was going to do. I held him, not caring if I crushed his bones, so long as I could just feel his heart.

"Dad, I'm so sorry, I…"

I didn't want to hear it.

I only wanted to savor this moment, this homecoming, this holding. It was too good to cloud it with words.

After a long, long, hug, and heaving tears, I stood back and focused on him. He looked awful: not an ounce of meat on his bones, and that gaunt, pained, sickly look on his face from too many drugs and too much fear.

But he was alive. And he was home.

"Let's get you inside," I said. "Your mother's got some coffee on."

The Prodigal, part 2

Scripture reference: Luke 15:11b–32

The first part of this parable is powerful enough. But the second takes it to a much richer level. It reminds us that our human relationships are never lived in a vacuum, but are intertwined with others in a wonderful, jumbled mess of life.

I knew the call would come, I just didn't know when. I wasn't prepared when it did.

"We have your daughter"—quick: is she dead or alive? "and we think you'd better come down. She was picked up for soliciting."

Was I allowed to feel relieved that she wasn't dead? Was I allowed to feel glad that she had been found? Was I allowed to feel all of the anger and frustration of three years that we had not heard from her?

I got in the car and drove through the fear of the night. It was late. It took two hours. That strange mix of adrenalin, pain, anger, fear, joy, and love propelled me down the road.

What would I say to her? What would she say to me?

It was far more awkward than I had imagined. There were no words. She looked like a walking cliché of cheap tart, painted and drugged, eyes hollowed by despair into glimpses of nothingness. My daughter.

Our hug was uncomfortable, forced. She seemed too scared to let herself go into my arms, and so it was business-like, strangely appropriate.

My questions were buried under an avalanche of silence. I couldn't ask them. Not yet. Maybe never.

I wanted to know, and I didn't want to know. I was probably as scared as she was.

They kept her—there was a fog of technicalities about jurisdiction and stuff that I couldn't understand.

The drive home took much longer.

We were allowed to visit her twice a week, and so we did. Drove two hours there, and two hours back, for one hour in a room full of a bunch of nervous people. All the way there we would convince ourselves it was better than nothing; on the way home we didn't talk much.

It became less uncomfortable over time. She began to look a bit better. Each week her smile dared to come back a little more. We found we could joke about a few things.

We still didn't ask all of the questions we wanted, but they somehow got answered little by little as heart threads reconnected.

One night we got home late, and I went into the kitchen to make myself a sandwich. Our other daughter Susan was just coming in from an evening out.

"How was your day?" I asked.

"Fine." She said. Then added for effect, "as if you care."

"What do you mean? Of course I care." Check: did I sound too defensive?

"Yeah, right. You're never here."

Calm.

Be calm.

Don't yell. Don't let all of that tension out. She doesn't deserve it.

I breathed.

"I…"

"You spend all your time off visiting that little slut."

I wanted to yell. But by the grace of God, I didn't, and in that micro-second, Susan started to cry.

"It's not fair," she said.

"I know. But she's your sister, and I love her."

Suddenly the air in the kitchen felt heavy.

"And I love you, too," I continued. "For the last three years I've had the privilege of watching you become a woman. I've gone to your basketball games and cheered like an idiot. I drove you to school when you missed the bus. I watched the fashion show when you bought all those clothes with your first paycheck. I've been worried when you stayed out late, and relieved when you came in, knowing you were safe and had been laughing with your friends.

"All of this, Susan, and I've loved every minute of it. But I never knew where your sister was. I imagined the worst, had to love her from a distance, not knowing if she were alive or dead…"

My tears were hot.

Susan hugged me.

"I'm sorry, Dad," she said. And then added, "I love you."

Two World Leaders

(The Pharisee and the Tax Collector)

Scripture reference: Luke 18:9–14

The story of the tax collector and the Pharisee praying in the temple was in the lectionary right around the time of the 50th anniversary of the United Nations, and I was struck by the image of so many world leaders, with differing backgrounds and worldviews, gathered in one place. I imagined two of them coming out of the UN chapel, being met by a TV reporter.

Reporter: Here comes one of the world leaders now. Let's see if we can talk to him. Excuse me, we noticed you were praying in there. Can you tell us why you were praying?

Leader One:	Well, I thought it was important to put in an appearance. You know, the folks back home always get impressed with a bit of the old-time religion.
Reporter:	I see; so your prayer was just for show, then?
Leader One:	Oh no, not *just* for show. I did talk to God—had quite a lot to bend the Almighty's ear about, actually. You see, this week, I've had the opportunity to meet the leaders of many nations around the world. It gives you reason to be grateful. So I passed on my gratitude, told God how glad I was that I came from a good nation.
	I mean, compared to some of these others! We're not a bunch of godless communists like the Cubans, we're not over-run with terrorists like those folks in the Middle East, we don't have all that AIDS nonsense to deal with or the ethnic violence or all that other stuff. All in all, I think we're doing pretty well.
Reporter:	And that's what you said in your prayer?
Leader One:	Pretty much, yes.
Reporter:	Well, thank you for taking the time to talk with us.
Leader One:	Not at all—I like to talk with the press.
Reporter:	Here comes another one. Excuse me…
Leader Two:	Who, me?
Reporter:	Yes. Might we have a word with you?
Leader Two:	Well, I, I suppose so.
Reporter:	We're wondering why you went in there to pray today.

Leader Two:	Well, I try to pray every day, whenever I can. It doesn't really matter where—a chapel, a mosque, a synagogue, a church, the place isn't that important—just so long as I get a chance to spend some quiet time with God.
Reporter:	I see. And what did you pray about today?
Leader Two:	Well, I began by asking God for forgiveness.
Reporter:	Forgiveness. Really?
Leader Two:	Yes. You see, at this event I've had the opportunity to meet leaders from many nations, and that's always a learning experience. As I reflect on the state of the world, I realize that as humans we have made a lot of mistakes, and we need to ask forgiveness.
	We are often so arrogant as a nation, and like to pretend we are self-made, forgetting that without God, we are nothing. We try to hide the anger and violence in our land, the crime and the sickness, the racism and classism and poverty permeating so much of our daily living. We are intolerant of one another's differences, wracked with prejudice. There are many problems that we do not address—it seems we would much rather focus on the problems of others outside our nation, so that we don't have to address our own issues. It's tragic. And it's shameful.
	So I asked God to forgive us, and to make us humble as a nation, that we might be open to God's guidance and in that find our true strength and source of pride.
Reporter:	And did you thank God for anything while you were in there?

Leader Two: Oh yes, I thanked God for the gifts of forgiveness and openness. I gave thanks for the gifts of diversity and understanding, of compassion and dialogue. I gave thanks that our God believes in second chances, and third and fourth and hundredth and thousandth chances. And I gave thanks that God would continue to journey with us and guide us.

Reporter: Thank you very much for speaking with us.

Leader Two: You're welcome. Thanks for the opportunity to share. God bless you.

Reporter: Thank you. There you have it, folks. Hard to believe they're from the same country, isn't it?

Crowd Conversion

(Zacchaeus)

Scripture reference: Luke 19:1–10

As a child, the story of the tax collector, Zacchaeus always intrigued me. Perhaps part of it was the image of this short person climbing up a tree to see Jesus—I think children can relate to that part. There was also the moral we were readily given at the end of it, that a "bad" person became "good" after meeting Jesus.

But is that what the story is really about? The Greek text can be read differently. The word "if" in verse 8 suggests that perhaps Zacchaeus wasn't the bad guy that everyone thought he was. Instead, an equally valid translation allows for the interpretation that Zacchaeus is not a cheat at all, but someone of much higher moral character than he's ever been given credit for. Maybe the people who get converted in this story are the ones who have their perceptions challenged...

You likely already know who I am—my reputation always seems to precede me, and that's generally not been a good thing. People used to say I needed a big name like Zacchaeus to make up for being short. I used to laugh along with them about that. But over time, people stopped saying much directly to me at all.

It seems the only times I heard my name spoken, it was in someone else's conversation with some unprintable adjective placed in front of it. Occasionally someone spat it out to me directly, again usually in the midst of a string of insults.

Most of the time, though, people who saw me in the streets or in the marketplace didn't quite know what to do with me. It seems they could never quite look me in the eye. Instead, they'd give me a weary, pitiful glance and a tepid, half smile, as if to say "Hello, Zacchaeus. So sorry you're who you are. Wish things were different. Can't really be seen talking to you. Hope you're okay." And then they'd avert their eyes, praying that no one had actually seen them looking at this sorry excuse for a human being.

If anyone did talk to me, it was business-like and to the point, never any conversation. Oh how I longed for someone to simply ask me how I was doing! Even some banal small talk—how wonderful it would be just to have someone say "Beautiful day, isn't it?" or "Do you think the grain harvest will be good this year?"

But it never happened.

Not even my family wanted to admit that they knew me.

You have to understand, it wasn't always this way. I started out well liked; I used to be a people pleaser. My sister said it was on account of being short that I tried so hard to please others, to get them to notice me. Perhaps she's right. Only it never really worked for very long.

As a teenager I got a job running errands for the Romans—a few coins to carry messages around town, that sort of thing. The other kids would take their time, but I always hurried. It's not that I liked the Romans, you understand, I simply loved to get praise for doing a good job.

Some years later an opening came up in the tax department and I leapt at the opportunity. You see, tax collectors were paid by commission, and could charge as much overhead as they wanted. It was a great way to make a living. But on the other hand, people despised tax collectors—called them dirt. And I wanted to be liked.

So an idea came to me: become a tax collector, and be fair. That would be a switch.

I would pay the Romans the percentage they demanded, but I wouldn't charge as much commission as the others, and that way everybody would like me.

Fat chance.

Oh the Romans liked me, all right. Because my rates were lower, people always paid me on time, and so I turned in a nice hefty bundle to the administrator every month. But all my fellow Jews hated me, assuming I was as corrupt as all the others.

Cheat. Traitor. Snake.

Those were some of the nicer things they called me.

Just when I was ready to pack it in, I got promoted to chief tax collector for the whole district. More prestige with the Romans, I thought, but more contempt from my own people. Was it worth it?

One day, there was a big commotion in town. Seems this Jesus fellow, from Nazareth, was coming. I'd heard about him, he had quite a following. Apparently he talked about justice and fairness, and reclaiming our heritage as God's chosen people. He also talked about tolerance and acceptance, which interested me. I thought he might be worth checking out.

It was hot, dusty, and heavy in town that day. The crowd started gathering early and by the time Jesus arrived you couldn't get anywhere near the road. Wanting at least to catch a glimpse of him, I climbed up the nearest tree.

I was rather disappointed, to be honest: Jesus looked quite, well, ordinary.

People were crowding around him, waving, grasping at his clothes. He smiled and held first one hand, then another.

And then he noticed me up in the tree. I waved—didn't know what else to do, really—and he looked straight at me.

"You're Zacchaeus, aren't you? I've heard about you."

If I could have melted away I would have, but you can't really do that when you're up in a tree and there's a huge crowd around. So I decided to climb down and speak my piece. If Jesus wanted to dress me down in front of all these people, it was time to set the record straight.

"I don't care what you've heard," I said, "it's nothing but a pack of lies."

The crowd went silent.

"I've always charged less commission than the other tax collectors, and always given one half of my earnings to care for the poor."

Jesus didn't say a word so I just kept right on talking.

"What's more, on the rare occasions when I have accidentally cheated somebody, I've paid them back, four times over. But does anybody care about that? Nooo! They say that because I work for the Romans I'm a cheat, and a good-for-nothing, and if you've come here to tell me the same thing, you can save your breath—I've heard it all before."

Jesus smiled a gentle, little smile, reached out, and placed a hand on my shoulder. I was shaking.

"Zacchaeus," Jesus said, "I know how kind and fair you are. I've also heard that you make a wonderful fish stew, and I'm very hungry. Could you give my friends and me a little lunch and a place to sit down? We could use a rest."

I blushed, and tried to get my shocked face to cooperate for a smile.

"And as for your reputation," Jesus continued, his voice getting louder, so that everyone could hear. "All I know is that you are a child of Abraham who tries to live a good life. I'd be proud to call you my friend."

Now, I would never brag about my fish stew, but I will tell you that Jesus and his crew finished all I could make. *And* they ate my bread and cheese, and drank my wine, and we all had a few laughs. That evening in the market square a crowd gathered to hear Jesus tell stories. It was the most wonderful night of my life.

From that day on, people treated me with a new respect. "That's Zacchaeus," they'd say, "you know, the one that Jesus visited."

I even managed to convince a couple of others who worked for the Romans to plan strategy with me so we could do our jobs and satisfy the government without ripping people off; it's amazing how easy it is sometimes to be just and fair if you only put your mind to it.

I've come to realize what people mean when they say that they're saved. It's that sense of knowing that you belong, that God loves you and accepts you, and cares about you—despite what other people might think.

Salvation came to *me*, that day, in the person of Jesus of Nazareth. It came in the form of friendship.

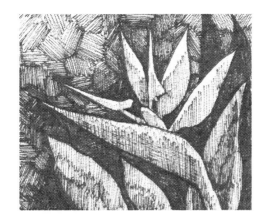

After the Wedding

(Jesus and Mary)

Scripture reference: John 2:1–11

There's no mistaking that Jesus got upset with Mary at the wedding at Cana—downright rude, actually, if one takes the Greek text at face value. And there's also no denying that Jesus had some anxiety, even doubt, about his ministry from time to time. I wondered if there might be some connection.

She was a mother; she was used to waiting. Waiting for him to be born. Waiting for him to learn to talk. Waiting for him to put toys away. Waiting for him to grow and become a man.

And the nights she had waited for him to come home—going to the window time after time, trying hard not to look obvious.

"Oh," she would say, if he caught her watching, worrying, "I was just checking to see if the rain had stopped."

But this time it was different.

He had never yelled at her like that before. And in front of their friends!

"Mind your own business!" he had shouted at her.

She wondered if he would dare to come home at all, or would he be too ashamed? All of these years, and he had never treated her like this.

At last, she heard the familiar sounds: the car in the driveway, the door slamming, the footsteps not so quiet on the stairs, the door opening.

She looked up; he seemed surprised to see her. (Surely he must have known she would have waited up?)

Softly, slowly, timidly, like a little boy, he approached her.

"Mother, I…"

"Why?" She interrupted. "Why did you have to be so rude to me? And in front of my friends?"

"I know. It was wrong. It's just that…"

"You're scared."

"How did you know?"

She allowed the gentle smile he knew so well to show through. "I'm a mother. It's my job."

"It's just that, I'm not ready."

"I remember having that same thought, about thirty years ago. Only that time it was during a visit from an angel, and I think you know what was being asked of me. And as you're well aware, I said 'yes.'"

"But it's different for me, mother. Once I begin, I'm in for the duration. It will be my whole life; there will be no turning back."

"And you think there was for me? You think that choosing to give birth to you, raising you, loving you, risking losing you—you don't think that's not *my* whole life? You don't think I'm as committed to your journey as you are? A parent is a parent forever, Jesus, not just for a little while."

"But what if I begin and I'm not ready?" Jesus said. "What then? Put a notice on the internet that says, 'Sorry, folks, we thought that the Reign of God was at hand, but it isn't. There's been a temporary disruption. Please log on again later'? I don't want to fail. I don't want to be some kind of joke."

"You won't fail. You can't fail. Just by being, you are a success. You know darned well that there are some—many—people who couldn't be bothered one way or another about the message you're going to bring.

And there are others who will be hostile to the core, because your words are going to challenge the very foundation of their corrupt living. Jesus, you know the stories of some of the ones who have gone before—it's not going to be a cakewalk, I'll grant you that. But it's who you are. We all have our paths—use the word destiny if you want—we all have our callings, and you can't deny it, not if you're going to be true to yourself. And that's all that God asks of any of us."

There was a pause.

"So," he said. "You think I'm ready, do you?"

"I do. You're old enough to have learned from your share of mistakes, but still young enough to ask questions. Still young enough to dare to do the foolish kinds of things you're going to have to do, to get your message across. I'm sure I'll have a lot more gray hair before you're done! No one will want to paint my portrait when I get old. But…you have to begin. God will make you ready."

"I suppose you're right. But, I'm still…"

"Scared. And that's okay. It's even healthy, from time to time."

There was another moment of silence.

"I guess it's time to start, then," he said.

Mary smiled. "Actually, I think you already did. I've had half a dozen phone calls about the wine, and it will be all over the papers tomorrow. Like it or not, you've pretty much begun."

"Yeah, well, I didn't have much choice, when you backed me into a corner."

"Oh, don't give me that, you still had a choice. When you told me off, you could have left. Like I've told you over and over again, don't blame anyone else for your choices."

"You're right, mother. And do you know how much that ticks me off?"

They both laughed. Mary grabbed her son and gave him a big hug.

"There's no turning back now, you know," Mary said. "But think of it: what a beginning, to show everyone the best time they've had in years. If we can convince people that the Reign of God is a celebration of life, and not a cloud of doom, then I think we're on the right track."

"What's this 'we' business, Mother?" Jesus asked.

"I told you, I'm in this as much as you are, you know. And so are your friends. It may be your road, but we'll go it with you. Who knows where it will lead?"

"Mother, you're wonderful." He hugged her again. "Just don't push me any more, okay?"

"Okay," she said. "I'll worry from time to time, but I won't push."

Born Again?

(Nicodemus)

Scripture reference: John 3:1–16

Nicodemus comes to see Jesus at night. Is it because he's fearful and needs the cover of darkness, or because he's been lying awake, trying to make sense of Jesus' teaching, and suddenly decides "I have to go and get some answers"? I wondered about the latter possibility, and this story was born of that wondering. And I wanted to push the conversation between Jesus and Nicodemus a little further, to see what might happen.

Nicodemus tossed and turned and tossed again. It was something the rabbi had said. Something about starting over.

"You must be born again," Jesus had said.

Well what the devil did that mean? It had seemed absolutely preposterous, so much so that Nicodemus' first reaction was to think Jesus was as crazy as all the other religious leaders thought he was. And yet…

And yet there was something that kept gnawing at him, something that kept pestering at the back of his mind, something that had kept Nicodemus from getting a decent night's sleep for over a week.

"You must be born again."

Finally he couldn't stand it any longer. "I have to know. I have to work this riddle out."

He fumbled around in the dark for his clothes, and made his way out the door.

"I have to know. I can't stand it. I'll wake him up if I have to."

Nicodemus realized it was not that late, and hoped that Jesus would still be awake. And when he found the place where Jesus and the others were staying, he saw candlelight flickering through the window. Nervously, he tapped on the door.

"Excuse me," he said timidly, "I'd like to speak with the rabbi."

Jesus looked up to see who the late night guest was, and smiled broadly when he recognized the council member, and motioned for him to come in.

"Master Nicodemus, this is a pleasant surprise. I thought I recognized you in the crowd the other day when I spoke in the town square. Now you come to pay me a visit. Tell me, what brings you out at this hour?"

"Rabbi, I believe you are a great teacher. I have listened to much of what you have to say, and I think you have a lot to offer our people. You teach simply and plainly—well, most of the time—and you speak the truth of God. But the other day you said something that's got me completely stymied. You said something about how we all needed to be born again. What on earth did you mean by that?"

Jesus' smile got even brighter.

"Ah, Nicodemus, I'm surprised you could not figure that one out, a wise teacher like yourself."

"But, good heavens, I'm an old man. I'll grant that it's probably a meta-phor, but what kind of metaphor? Perhaps a child could start over, but…how does a grown adult become reborn? It doesn't make sense."

"You know, Nicodemus, you're just like so many other religious lead-ers. You think with your head. Try thinking with your heart. It's precisely *because* you are so 'grown up' that you need to be born again. And don't worry, I'm not singling you out—we all need it. Not just once, either, but over and over and over again."

"Oh dear," Nicodemus shook his head and threw up his hands, "now you've completely lost me."

"Let me try and explain," Jesus said. "We all get born as human beings, out of the water of our mother's womb—that's a given. We grow, we learn, we decide how things are. But sometimes God has other ideas. As we get older, however, we seem to get more and more set in our ways. Along comes God's Spirit—like a refreshing wind—and rebirths us, sets us right again. That is, if we let it. We can be stubborn and refuse to hear it, refuse to feel it, deny that it's there.

"Have you ever tried to deny the wind on a blustery day, Nicodemus? That would be pretty silly, wouldn't it? It's the same thing with trying to deny God's Spirit. Sadly, there are people who do it. It will be blowing all around them, trying to rejuvenate them, fill them with new life, and they'll try their darnedest to pretend that it isn't there.

"Or worse still," Jesus continued, "there are those who think they know all about God's Spirit, think they can control it, as if they could control the wind. There are those who think they know all there is to know about God, as if God were finished with the world, as if God had nothing more to say to us, as if we were complete. Silly, really. But, if you're born of the Spirit, God guides you—here, there, everywhere."

"So I could be born again, and God's Spirit would guide me?" the old man asked.

"Absolutely," Jesus said. "And not just once, either. We only get one chance to be born physically. But spiritually—no limit at all. Because there are no limits to what God can do. You ought to know that, Nicodemus, you being a teacher yourself."

"Well, yes, but…" It was obvious that he needed some time to take it all in. They sat quietly for a while.

"It's not so difficult as you think," Jesus said, breaking the silence. "Another way to put it is to think of it as being born from above—born as a child of God. We all *are* children of God, but sometimes we forget that. And, when we do, we get to be reborn, and can remember all over again that we are God's children."

Jesus paused again, realizing that Nicodemus needed another moment to let this last bit sink in. Then Jesus continued,

"No one can recognize the reign of God without being born again. And yet, my friend, you see it, don't you?"

Nicodemus hesitated. "I'm not sure."

"Why did you come here tonight?" Jesus asked.

"Because I wanted to know more of what you were teaching. I wanted to try to understand some of what you had said the other day. I wanted to make sense of it." Nicodemus began to sound just a little bit defensive.

"I think there's maybe a little more to it than that," Jesus offered. "I think you are beginning to realize that God's reign is happening even here, even now. I think that, unlike some of your fellow teachers and leaders, you're beginning to understand the scriptures a little more clearly. You're sensing that the reign of God isn't something to hope for and dream about and pray for that might happen later on, in a place far, far away, after we die. I believe you're recognizing that it is here, it is now.

"And *that,*" Jesus declared, "suggests to me that you may be being reborn, Nicodemus, at least a little bit."

Nicodemus looked straight at Jesus. "I don't know that I would go that far."

"Oh, don't worry," Jesus said, "I'm not accusing you of anything. And I'm not about to go running in the streets telling people. It's your business, my friend, yours and God's—not mine."

"I really don't know about all of this." Nicodemus was beginning to feel less comfortable, less sure, than he had been.

"You don't have to *know,*" Jesus said, "you just have to believe it, to feel it. Understanding can come later. Much later. If ever, frankly."

"Even so," Nicodemus said. "I don't know that I'm quite ready to embrace all of what you're saying. I am intrigued, to be sure, but I don't know that I'm ready to let go of all I have been taught. You're asking me to set aside teachings of my elders—of your elders, of our elders—and grab a hold of something completely new here."

"Is it new? Or is it what was there all along? All I'm doing, Nicodemus, is inviting you to think on these things. I have not come to pass judgment—on you or anybody else. Rather, I am here to offer the world a new way of understanding God, a new way of being with God. Because that's really what God wants in all of this. All of the laws, all of the Torah, all of our prayers, all of the things we do—they are all for one purpose, to bring us closer to God. For when we are closer to God, we are more likely to do the will of God, the one who made us, and birthed us, and loves us. Above all else, remember that, Nicodemus: God loves us."

There was another silence, a bit more awkward this time. It seemed as if both men knew the conversation had reached its conclusion.

"Rabbi, I thank you," Nicodemus said. "I came with a question, and I leave with many more. You have given me much to think upon."

"I pray that I have been helpful," Jesus said, "and that I have not simply made things more confusing for you."

"I'm not sure," Nicodemus replied. "I'm not sure. I must go back, and reflect upon these things. I fear that I shall have a few more sleepless nights before I figure it all out."

Pilate's Report

(Holy Week)

Scripture reference: Matthew 21:1–17; Matthew 26:57–27:66; Mark 11:1–11, 15–17; Mark 14:53–15:47; Luke 19:28–48; Luke 22:63–23:55; John 12:12–19; John 18:1–19:42

One thing that attracts me to this story is the irony that Pilate, who had all the might of Rome behind him (in other words, what was perceived as all of the power in the world) is overwhelmed by a conversation with this itinerant rabbi, and intimidated by the leaders of this "backward" nation. I think that Pilate was profoundly shaken by his encounter with Jesus, and that intrigues me.

So I imagined Pilate filing a report with the superiors in Rome, trying to explain the unexplainable, and trying more than anything else to simply cover his backside.

Your Imperial Excellency,

As you have requested, I offer here an explanation of recent events concerning the Galilean preacher Jesus, and my response to this situation. I can assure you that I tried to follow the letter of the law to the utmost degree, and ask that you not judge me too harshly. It is no simple task to govern these people.

If I might be so bold as to offer a quick summation, the man was quite simply a lunatic. By way of background, it may interest you to know that, despite repeated warnings from his own followers, as well as other leaders within the Jewish community, this man chose to come directly to Jerusalem and challenge Roman authority.

Like yourself, I couldn't care less for abuses of Jewish law—their fanatical obsession with detail can make even our Roman thoroughness seem lax at times. However, when such abuses threaten to disturb the peace or, more precisely, encourage rebellion amongst the people, then I am most eager to defend our authority immediately.

Last Sunday this man rode into Jerusalem on the back of a donkey, in blatant mockery of an imperial procession. The crowd dared to hail him as a ruler (he has variously claimed to be a descendant of the old King David, although this lineage has not been established and, to his credit, the man does not seem to have quite the delusions of grandeur that his followers would want to bestow upon him). Nevertheless, in this instance Jesus seemed to make no effort to stop them.

You must understand, too, that these are very volatile times. The annual Passover festival is ripe for nationalistic fervor and potential terrorist attacks. It only takes one crazy fool to set them all off, I can assure you.

In the middle of the week, this Jesus went into their Temple—it was positively swarming with pilgrims from all over the Empire—and went completely berserk, overturning furniture, intimidating the traders, ranting uncontrollably and even, by at least one account, beating people with a whip. This fracas required the involvement of two full divisions of my men to restore order, and has incurred the wrath of the entire business community, who have been most persistent in their complaints. Damage estimates are in the hundreds of thousands, and almost a full day of commerce had to be suspended—you can well imagine the ramifications. And, of course, Rome is being blamed for everything, due to our promise to keep the peace. All of this, caused by one insolent little rebel.

You can only imagine my desire, then, to meet this brute and thus I am sure you will be as surprised as I was to learn that he is (or, I suppose, more precisely *was*) a rather unassuming character, quite subdued and quiet in my presence and yet, strangely, not frightened. Dazed, perhaps, and confused, surely, but not frightened. Not intimidated at all.

My first reaction, when he was brought to me early in the morning, was to feel sorry for the poor fellow. I wanted to take him in and offer him a meal—he looked more like a discarded rag doll than a revolutionary leader. He elicited first my pity, later my frustration, and finally my disgust. Yet at no time did he draw out my hatred or my anger; he simply did not seem worth it.

The Jews went on and on about him breaking this law and that law—infantile stuff about medicine show antics on their Sabbath and such like; pointless stuff, really. However, some fairly credible witnesses did offer evidence of inciting to riot, claims to royal authority, and apparently at least one incident of urging people not to pay their taxes.

My immediate thought was to hold a quick trial, reminding the accused of just what he could expect if he tried to cross Roman authority in future, and then let the silly beggar go, but the local leaders would hear none of it.

Oh no, they wanted him put to death. Apparently he had blasphemed their god, and they would not settle for anything less than execution. Now, I am a tolerant man, as you well know, and I like to support local authority when it seems politic, but in this instance, I thought they were using a rather large hammer to destroy a rather insignificant pest. But you should have seen them! Quite hostile, and most insistent. One has to admire their devotion to their convictions, I suppose.

We talked back and forth a short while, and then I brought Jesus in for questioning.

"Are you the King of the Jews?" I asked, trying to ignore the humor of the situation—he could hardly have looked less like a king if he had tried.

"Why do you want to know?" he retorted.

"I don't want to know at all. *I* know who you are. I simply wondered if *you* know who you are. Your own people have turned you in. Doesn't that tell you something?"

"I am not a king in the way you think of the word. If I were, I would be sitting where you are now," he replied.

"Ah, so you are a king?"

"If that's what you wish to call me. But where you rule with the might and power of Rome behind you, I am armed only with the truth."

"Is that so?" I asked. "And just what do you mean by that?"

He said nothing. Absolutely nothing. He only looked at me.

I can assure you, your Excellency, that the stories claiming I was visibly shaken are false. I was simply insulted. The man was pathetic.

I told him that I had the power to set him free, that I could let him go on about his silly business, but he said nothing. Not a word. I had a good mind to release him, but his rudeness started to get to me. Not an ounce of respect for my position, for our authority.

Still, out of pity, I gave him one more chance—I would let the crowd decide.

You may know that it is customary, in keeping with the Jewish concern for compassion, to release a prisoner at the Passover festival. So, I offered up Jesus and another nasty piece of work called Barabbas. I felt sure that they would want Jesus to go free and watch Barabbas writhe in agony on a cross for all he had done, but I was quite wrong. The whole of the assembled crowd seemed almost possessed as they shouted for the release of Barabbas, and screamed for the blood of Jesus. What choice did I have? I washed my hands of the whole affair, and ordered the soldiers to take Jesus away for crucifixion.

I can make no comment on the behavior of my men at this point, except to say that, as I am sure you can well understand, it is quite a common occurrence for the guards to vent some of the tension of their work by having a bit of harmless fun with the condemned before they finish them off. I can, however, assure you that their mockery of Jesus' royal status in no way impinged on the dignity of Rome.

As for the sign denoting Jesus as "King of the Jews," I in no way meant it as an insult to your Excellency or to our Divine Augustus. I can only say that I was caught up in the moment. Rumors that I had been drinking heavily are also quite false. I suppose if anything I wanted to show to the Jewish people that their so-called king was a naked, dirty, powerless man breathing out his last moments in pointless agony on a Roman cross. I wanted to remind them where the real power in this world lies.

I feel quite certain that this problem has been suitably contained, and you need not concern yourself with the rumors you may have heard of some sort of ongoing cult. I assure you that we have matters well in hand. Unfortunately, there will be other minor threats to our authority in this land—these are, after all, a most stubborn people as you well know. However, I am confident that none of them will amount to any more than this one, whose memory will dry up as readily as morning dew. Consider the matter at an end.

I am your humble and respectful servant,
Pilate,
Governor of Judea.

Mary Magdalene's Legacy

Scripture reference: John 20:11–18

One of the most liberating, life-giving stories for me is the encounter of Mary Magdalene and the risen Christ in the garden of the empty tomb. I think it is for many others as well, given the enormous popularity—at least in North America—of the hymn "In the Garden" that retells this story. In complete and utter despair, Mary finds her life, her hopes, and her dreams in tatters. And then Christ appears to her again…

You have called me a whore
from the very beginning,
for two thousand years now
and Eve before me:
called us all whores
and witches
and worse.

You never bothered
to get to know me;
never wanted to ask me:
        why are you alone?
        what is your story?
        who are you, really?
        how are you feeling?

The other disciples
from the twelve
through countless thousands
have discredited me
discredited us
called me a liar
a trouble-maker
a disruption
a nuisance
and worse.

I frustrate you.
I confound you.
For two thousand years
you have quietly
(and not so quietly)
wished I would go away.

When the others turned and fled
the cross,
and the tomb,
did you think I would flee, too?
Did you think I would give up?
How could I?

My life was too entangled with his.
(Oh no, I won't satisfy your cheap curiosity
with titillating gossip
and spill the beans here)
No details
except to say that
had you not been so afraid of other's stories
you might have learned a little more about not only me
but other disciples who ministered along-side Jesus,
learned of the work of so many more:
the women, the children, the also-rans.

But all that aside,
I never could have fled.
Despite all I endured
for three days,
for two thousand years,
I had to stay.

And in the silence,
in the waiting,
Christ came.
And louder than all of the scorn
        and the ridicule
        and the fear
        and the hatred,
louder than all of the lies
        and the misunderstandings
        and the abuse
        and the mistrust

Christ spoke my name:

        "Mary."

And I experienced resurrection.

It is that same Christ who commissioned me
to go and tell.

So I am here—
I have not gone away,
I *will* not go away.
As long as anyone, anywhere, is
        rejected
        cast aside
        spat upon
by the world—or,
worse still,
        by the church—
I am here
to proclaim the same truth
once told to me:
Christ Jesus is risen for you,
and calls you by name.

Let no one
        no one
ever tell you otherwise.

Included

(Philip and the Ethiopian Official)

Scripture reference: Acts 8:26–40

The Ethiopian official is more generally known as the "eunuch," defined by a physical deformity that placed him outside of the community of God's people, forbidden by scripture from even worshipping in the temple. As such, I have often seen him in this story as representing all those who have been told by the church that they do not belong, and I invite them to place themselves in this person's story.

The torrential rain had delayed several flights, leaving the airport lounge more crowded than usual. Philip gingerly made his way across an assortment of legs, children, backpacks, and briefcases to the one empty seat.

"May I?" he asked the well-dressed man whose bag was occupying the chair.

"Oh sure," the man replied, moving the bag. "Sorry about that."

"No worries." Philip set his own backpack on the floor and sat down. "Thanks."

"Don't mention it," the man said. And as an after thought he stretched out his hand, "my name's Jonathan, by the way."

"Nice to meet you. I'm Philip."

"Listen, Philip, would you mind watching my stuff for a minute while I…?" he nodded in the direction of the restroom.

"Not at all. You go ahead."

Jonathan set down the book he had been reading and headed off. A few minutes later he returned.

"Thanks. I appreciate that. It saves having to take everything with me."

"I understand," Philip said. "I hope you don't mind, I took a look at the book you're reading. Look's interesting."

"It is," Jonathan said. Then he added, "kind of. Frankly, it's a little heavy going. I picked it up at the bookstore at the big church downtown. I've read a lot of spiritual stuff, but this one…I don't know; I'm having trouble getting into it."

"Interested in religion are you?" Philip inquired.

"Well, not really 'religion.' More spirituality, I suppose. I think I'm what you call a 'seeker.' I've probably read every book on spirituality, and every self-help book, and every book on how to discover the real you and heal your inner child and, you name it, I've read it."

"And has it worked? Have you found the real you?"

"Not really," Jonathan said. "Somebody told me that if I stopped searching I'd discover I wasn't really lost but, when I tried that, it didn't help. So I keep reading. But…I haven't found the answers yet. I've read every eastern religion out there, read all the pop psychologists, all the new age, old age, in between age—don't seem to have found the key yet."

"What drew you to this one? Did you go to a service at the church or something?"

Jonathan chuckled a little. "Hardly. I'm not really a church kind of guy. If you want to know the truth, I went to check out the architecture. I'd heard that it was quite a beautiful building, and that's why I went. On Saturday. I haven't felt welcome in a church on a Sunday for years."

"That's a shame," Philip said.

Jonathan detected—and appreciated—a note of compassion in Philip's voice.

"Yeah, I guess it is," Jonathan said. Part of him couldn't believe he was having this conversation with a complete stranger. Yet another part of him was so very grateful for the opportunity to revisit a story that had been lingering untold for too long.

"You see," Jonathan continued, "I grew up in the church. Sunday school, Christmas pageants, summer church camp, the whole bit. I thought I belonged, you know? I learned these stories about God, and Jesus, and we were taught that someday we would give our lives to Jesus, and he would enter our hearts, and I kept waiting for the special feeling." Jonathan paused, and offered a slight laugh. "I actually thought I would physically feel Jesus entering my heart. You know, through my chest. Never happened.

"Anyway, the other kids kept having this experience of being 'saved' and I hoped, prayed it would happen to me. I knew that if I were just good enough, prayed hard enough, it would happen. Even though...I wondered. I worried. Deep down, maybe I never could be good enough. One year at camp, the others were having these wonderful born again experiences, and being baptized, and I wanted it so badly. And then..." Jonathan hesitated, drew a long breath, and slowly let it out.

"And then, I told one of the other kids that I thought I was gay. Everything stopped. The youth group leader let it be known that in God's eyes I was not acceptable. I was out of the youth group, and out of the church—end of story."

There was a brief moment of silence between the two men.

"So, I guess that's why I keep reading all of these books. I'm trying to find a story where I fit in."

"Well," Philip offered, "despite anything that youth group leader may have told you, or any preacher may have told you, I think I know the story where you fit. Can I tell it to you?"

Jonathan glanced outside for a moment; it was still raining hard. "Sure. It looks like we won't be going anywhere for a while."

And so Philip began to tell a story. It was a story of a God who created a world and declared it good. Of a God who heard the cries of people in slavery and brought them to freedom. Of a God who made covenant after covenant after covenant with people, and said "I cannot give you up; I will always love you."

And Philip told of someone named Jesus who invited women and men and children to gather at table and break bread. Of Jesus who said "whoever is without sin, cast the first stone." Of Jesus who challenged people to welcome and love even those who seemed outside the circle, who were different, who felt they did not belong. Of Jesus who told stories about welcoming even when to do so tried and tested every fiber of our being.

"The story doesn't end," Philip said. "It is an ongoing story, and you and I are a part of it. Jesus came to bring people into God's story, not push them out. Jesus came to make sure that there was room enough at the table for all of God's children. *All* of them, Jonathan. That includes you. You are welcome in the church because you are part of the family of God."

"But..." Jonathan began.

"No buts," Philip said. "You belong. Like it says in that song you probably learned years ago in Sunday school, Jesus loves you—the Bible says so. Unconditionally. You belong, Jonathan."

"Wow," Jonathan said. "I have to tell you that, after all these years, for once I really believe it. Those stories that you're telling me, they're not new. I've read them before, I've heard them before, but they didn't click before. Now hearing them this way, this time, for some reason, Philip, things are falling into place. It's amazing! To think all the money I wasted on those darned books, when it was the story I'd already learned—I just didn't *get* it before."

"That's okay," Philip said.

"I know," Jonathan said. "I know. It's just...I want to make up for lost time. It's so incredible to feel like I finally belong. It's like...okay, I know this is going to sound silly. In fact...no, it's too weird."

"What?"

"It's just that, after hearing everything you said, and feeling at last like I belong and everything, I wish I could be baptized. I know, I told you, it's crazy."

"It's not crazy at all," Philip said. "When you get home, I think…"

"No, I mean now," Jonathan interrupted. "I wish I could get baptized now. That's why it's crazy."

Philip paused for a moment. And then, as if on cue, both men noticed the water fountain in the corner of the airport lounge. They looked at each other.

"Are you thinking what I'm thinking?" Jonathan asked.

"I think so," Philip said.

"Why not?"

"Yeah, why not?"

They got up and went to the fountain. They quickly looked around and then, without even taking a second to work out any logistics or liturgical formula, Philip pressed the button and the water shot up and Jonathan closed his eyes and dunked his head, and Philip said, "Jonathan, child of God, I baptize you in the name of the One who created you and loves you always. Amen."

Jonathan shook his head, and opened his eyes.

"Whoa, that was…" he began, but he noticed that Philip was no longer standing beside him. He turned, first left, then right, but Philip was nowhere to be seen.

For a fleeting moment, Jonathan wondered, had he imagined it? The whole thing was silly enough, perhaps it was a dream?

Except it couldn't be, because he felt so completely alive, so completely transformed.

That, and the fact that his hair was wet.

The Sin Thing

(Romans 7 and 8)

Scripture reference: Romans 7:7–8:1

How to define and understand sin, and grace? Paul struggles with it in many of his writings. We struggle with it in our daily living. I think that when we join Paul in the wondering, discerning, and struggling, we can learn far more than if we try to take Paul's writing as "law" which is frankly pretty ironic.

Oh how I struggle with this. I struggle with this day and night. I wish I had the answers. I have only one answer: the grace of Jesus Christ. I just wish I could make sense of it sometimes. I want to *understand* it.

The Torah, *that* I understood. I studied it. I knew it backwards and for-wards, in my sleep even. I could recite the Torah standing on my head. You wanted to know the rules? I could tell you the rules. Problem is, I couldn't live by them. And that was a big problem.

I suppose, had I never studied the Torah, I would have been free as a bird. Funny, you know, I never thought of it that way! If I'd never learned about sin, would I have been innocent of it all? Oh well, too late now, I suppose. I *did* learn about it. So I have no excuse.

I learned what God wanted of me. I *knew* what God wanted of me, and I didn't do it. Couldn't do it. Could any of us? Good heavens, from Adam and Eve on down the line, we've all been making mistakes. We can't help it—it's what we do. And God knows it, obviously, or else God wouldn't have given us the Torah.

And I'm not faulting the Torah, either. It is a blessed gift from God, and has guided us for so long. I just can't live up to it.

For sin is the problem. Sin—that tragic state of being distanced from God. That's the problem. The reality that, left to my own devices, given the choice, I'd rather do things my way than God's way. And, when I do that, I end up farther and farther away from God.

Do I like that fact? Of course not! I hate it, if you want to know the truth.

That's why I studied the Torah for so long. That's why I clung to it as if it were hard and fast rules, hoping against hope that if I could only follow it to the letter, it would bring me closer to God. And I can't fault those who thought the same thing. I can't fault those who want to try anything reasonable to get closer to God and travel in God's ways. It's just that I've become convinced that it doesn't work. Can't work. Because, ultimately, *we* can't do it. No matter how hard we try.

I've learned this the hard way, friends. And perhaps you have, too. I think it's human nature. And I'm only human. You are, too. I have the best of intentions, but by default, in comes sin. Now, I know, we all like to say "the devil made me do it" but we don't have the luxury of that cheap excuse, cute though it may be. I have no one to blame but myself. When I don't stay in touch with God, I rely too much on myself. And that's the problem.

Left to my own devices, I follow my own best intentions. And, well, lovely though they may be, they're mine. And while I might like to think I have all the answers, I don't.

My agenda is nothing compared to God's. I'm powerless, compared to God. I want to do what is right, but I'm hopeless. I'm dreadful at it.

It doesn't mean I'm a bad person, it just means I'm a disaster at running my own life—let alone anyone else's—without God's guidance. Trying to do it by myself, or trying to do it by simply following some set of static rules simply isn't going to cut it. And if I do try to live that way—by a set of rules—I'm doomed to failure before I start. That leads to guilt, and that, in turn, gets me nowhere, just farther and farther from God.

No, if I'm going to get anywhere in this world—I'm talking in God's world, now, not in terms of being an earthly "success story"—I have to let go. I have to give up Paul's agenda and get on board with God's agenda.

Easy? I don't think so.

I struggle. I have to admit that I'm powerless, and let go and let God, as they say.

And the key to the whole puzzle?

Jesus Christ.

God's living Torah, if you will. The spirit of Jesus Christ sets us free from our own rules, and the world's rules, and allows us to travel with God. All we have to do is let go and allow Christ to guide us. I know, I know, much easier said than done.

But I find that when I do open myself to Christ, even just a little bit, amazing things can happen. And God makes no judgments against us—God's patience in this regard is quite amazing. Open up a little bit, and God does the rest.

If only I could remember to do it on a daily basis, I'd be set!

Dare to Love

(1 Corinthians 13)

Scripture reference:　　　　　1 Corinthians 13

This piece was originally used in a specific worship setting, at a specific time in history. Yet I think that much of its message still works.

One of the things that always intrigued me about this scripture text is the reference to thinking like a child. Maybe we've been misunderstanding Paul all these years; maybe there is a twinge of sadness that he has had to "put away childish things..."

What if I could stand up here and say the most wonderful things,
　　　and sound impressive
　　　and answer everyone's questions
but I didn't love anyone: what would be the point?

What if we were the most incredible church
　　　where every pew was filled,

the preaching was always inspirational,
the choir always sang perfectly,
and we served the best coffee in town,
but no one felt loved: what would be the point?

What if as a community we taught our children
    lots of data and knowledge
    so they could recite the books of the Bible
    (backwards *and* forwards)
    and know all the right words
but they didn't know how to love? What have they really learned?

If we are thrilled to have a day off of work
to honor the birth of the prophet Martin Luther King
    and yet we don't do anything to alleviate poverty
    racial inequality
    sexism and homophobia
    injustice and oppression
in this community, in our workplaces, in our schools,
in our homes and in our churches,
    what have we gained?

If we put Mother Theresa of Calcutta on a pedestal
    and revere her as a saint,
    admire her from a distance,
    and yet do not feed and clothe the hungry and the naked,
    do not care for the sick and the dying,
    do not provide basic health care to all our people,
where is the honesty in that?

In short: if we don't love, what's the point?

Love is: good.
Love is: Christ-like.

Love is kind, and patient,
    love is trusting.
Love is the opposite of fear.

If we remember that God's love triumphs in the end—
       if we really believe that—
   then we can trust God,
   we can dare to dream.
   We can dare to live
as God's people.

Love always wants what's best,
even for the other person.

Love cheers for both sides in the great football game of life,
    and says, "let just have fun together;
      it doesn't matter who wins."

Love is always supportive.
Love turns things around.
Love takes hopeless situations and lets us see hope in them.
Love enables us to move mountains,
break down walls,
and plant flowers in the midst of pavement.
Love never,
    ever,
ends.

Oh, other things will end:
    fads and fashions will go out of date;
    rules will change;
    computers will do more and more
    (and become obsolete faster and faster).

The scenery will change.
But the world will not come to an end.

We may even give up,
    but God's love will continue,
and what is perfect will someday appear,
and what is not perfect will disappear,
and the world will turn and turn and turn
and keep on turning,
whether we even notice or not.

You know, when I was a small child,
    I looked at the world with a child-like wonder:
    I trusted, dreamed, imagined, hoped.
Then I grew up.
I became "practical,"
    cynical.
Now all I can understand about God's ways
    is what my grown-up mind will let me.
But when I allow my inner child
    to listen to God's voice,
    and to really live,
I'm not so scared any more.
I have a sense that things can work out,
and I trust that one day, someday,
I *will* see God face to face.
One day I *will* understand things,
just like God does now.

But for now, I don't need to know all that.
I don't need to know everything.
I don't need to understand everything.
I don't need answers to all of life's questions.
I don't have to wait until I'm older

(or wish I were younger).
I don't have to wish I were taller or shorter
    or even more good-looking.
I just have to try,
    try to do what God wants of me.
and stop looking for excuses.

I just have to remember that there are three things in life
that really matter:
    faith
    hope
    and love.

and the greatest of these
    is love.

Study guide

Wonderful things can happen when we discuss the Bible with others. We learn new things: about the Bible, about one another, about God, about life, and about ourselves. It can be challenging, fun, thought-provoking, scary, exciting (sometimes all at once!) and a host of other things besides. Here are some suggestions for using this book in group discussion.
(Suggestions for individual study are included at the end of this general section.)

GUIDELINES

Group norms

Before you begin, it's good to establish some group norms. Agree to these at the outset. You will probably want to include things such as these:

- Respect one another.

- Each person's experience and beliefs are welcome.

- This group is not about converting one another, but about sharing and learning together. Disagreement is allowed, even encouraged.

- All questions are welcome. There can be more than one answer to almost all of life's questions. There are no "dumb" questions.

- We all have things we can learn from one another. We all have things we can teach one another.

- People have the right to speak and to be heard, or to be silent.

- When we talk about faith issues, people can have strong opinions, and people are often at different places on faith journeys. All are welcome.

It is also important to agree on the level of confidentiality that people are anticipating in the group. Some participants may be hesitant to share about their faith or to offer opinions on the Bible without an assurance that others will respect that things shared in the group stay in the group. Similarly, it can be devastating to share a very personal experience in the context of a biblical discussion, in what one assumes is a safe and confidential situation, only to hear it discussed elsewhere, even by someone with the best of intentions. Establishing a clear understanding of what is to remain within the group and what can be discussed elsewhere helps to avoid uncomfortable situations.

Size of group

An ideal group size is somewhere between about four and ten. More than that becomes quite unwieldy and difficult for discussion. If you do have more than ten, it's best to divide into smaller groups so that everyone gets a chance to share.

Supplies

This will depend on the type of study you will be doing. At the very least, every participant will need a copy of this book. (Please do not photocopy—it's both illegal and unethical. Thanks.) Also, everyone should have a Bible. If possible, bring a variety of translations and, if you'd like, some storytelling versions.

Everyone tends to have their favorite translations. Some that I would recommend would be the *New Revised Standard Version* (generally accepted as the most accurate, and scholarly, translation); *Today's New International Version* (highly readable, accurate, and more inclusive than its predecessor); *Contemporary English Version* (probably the most readable modern translation); *New Jerusalem Bible* (considered by many to have the best "flow").

It is also a good idea to have some paraphrase or story versions of the Bible. In this category I would place both the *King James Version* and *The Message*. The former because, while a landmark of English literature, it is simply not very accurate and, well, we don't speak that kind of English any more, and so it is constantly prone to misinterpretation and misunderstanding. Although it sounds lovely, don't use it as a study Bible, use it as a story Bible.

Eugene Peterson's *The Message* is one of my absolute favorites, and I use it frequently. It is, however, a paraphrase and not a translation. Great for comparison purposes, but I would not recommend it as the sole Bible for study purposes.

If your group wants to explore a Bible passage in depth, it can help to have a commentary handy, although I caution against having too many resources or a) the study gets bogged down really quickly and b) some people can feel very inadequate. A good Bible dictionary can be helpful for explanation of general things. Many study Bibles have quick reference materials that can help answer a lot of simple questions about background. And, if someone or the group wants to know more than the group can answer, it's perfectly okay to say "hmm. Not sure about that. Would someone like to do a little research and let us know next week?"

Having paper and pens available will be helpful if your group is going to do some writing. One of the options each week is to write your own version of the story. Similarly, depending on your group it may be helpful to have a large writing surface (whiteboard, newsprint, etc.) and markers available. You never know when someone wants to write or draw something for the group—it's always helpful to be prepared.

Background

The stories in this book are different than other Bible stories. They have been intentionally rewritten from a different angle, with some kind of "twist." Presumably, that intrigued you when you purchased the book. However, in a group study, that could be unnerving for some folk. They may not be used to looking at Bible stories in ways other than how they first heard them, or first had them explained to them.

In this case, it can be helpful to offer some introductory or background material. A resource that I would highly recommend is Marcus Borg's *The Heart of Christianity* (HarperSanFrancisco, 2004). You could simply suggest that group members read the book. Or you could first do an in depth exploration of the book using the 12-session study guide *Experiencing the Heart of Christianity* by Tim Scorer (Wood Lake Books, 2005).

If you do not want to take the time to do the full study, the third session ("The Bible: the Heart of the Tradition") gives an excellent introduction to new ways of understanding and experiencing the Bible. Using the study guide—which includes a brief DVD clip of Marcus Borg speaking about ways of understanding the Bible as metaphor—to lead a one-session introduction to Bible study (frankly, any Bible study) can be of great value. I cannot recommend this book highly enough.

Borg's *Reading the Bible Again for the First Time* (HarperSanFrancisco, 2001) is also a very helpful resource in this regard.

STUDY SESSION OUTLINE

1. Welcome participants *(make sure everyone knows each other's name)*.

2. Establish or review group norms/familiarize newcomers with group norms.

3. Pray.

4. Read the scripture passage *(listed above the specific story to be explored)*.

5. Brief discussion on the scripture passage *(sharing insights, queries, general background)*.

6. **Option:** guided meditation *(see suggestions in box for leading guided meditation)*. You may prefer to do the guided meditation later, or you may wish to do it both times. For some stories, it will work better after the story—in other instances, it can work either time.

7. Read the introduction to the story *(the portion in italics)*.

8. Read the story. Either invite one person to read the story, or assign parts to narrator and various characters as appropriate. If possible, give people an opportunity to prepare ahead of time.

9. Discuss the story with these general questions.

    a. What new insights has this story brought out for you?

    b. How has it helped you to understand the original biblical passage?

    c. How has it challenged you in your understanding of the original biblical passage?

    d. What questions did it raise for you?

    e. How might you retell the story?

10. Discuss the story using the additional specific questions for that story listed below.

11. a. ***Option:*** invite people to spend some time writing their own version of the story. Provide an opportunity for people to read their stories afterwards, if they wish.

    b. ***Option:*** guided meditation *(see suggestions in box for leading guided meditation).*

12. Close with prayer or a hymn.

Guided meditation
Note: when leading this, to ensure pauses of a sufficient length, silently count from one to five slowly during each pause. During the meditation, use the biblical character's names, rather than "he" or "she" or "they."
Get in a comfortable position and close eyes your eyes. Take two or three deep breaths in and out. *(pause)*
Imagine that you are present in the story we just read. You can see *(name)*. What does *(name)* look like? *(pause)*
How old is *(name)*? *(pause)*
What kind of expression does *(name)* have? *(pause)*
(name) speaks to you—what does *(name)* say? *(pause)* What do you want to say to *(name)* in return?

GUIDELINES FOR INDIVIDUAL STUDY

1. Read the scripture passage *(listed above the specific story to be explored).*

2. ***Option:*** guided meditation *(see suggestions in box for leading guided meditation).* You may prefer to do the guided meditation later, or you may wish to do it both times.

3. Read the introduction to the story, and the story.

4. Reflect on these general questions:

   a. What new insights has this story brought out for you?

   b. How has it helped you to understand the original biblical passage?

   c. How has it challenged you in your understanding of the original biblical passage?

   d. What questions did it raise for you?

   e. How might you retell the story?

5. Reflect on the additional specific questions for that story listed below.

6. ***Option:*** you may wish to write your own version of the story.

7. ***Option:*** guided meditation—you may wish to repeat this activity.

SPECIFIC DISCUSSION QUESTIONS

Sarah's Laughter

- When have you been shocked—or confused, angry, devastated, frustrated—with life's turns of events, and turned to God in bewilderment? When have these emotions turned to laughter? What was the process?

- Do you tend to think that God has plans for our lives, or do you tend to think that strange things happen, and God somehow works through them? Or is life a mixture of both?
- What have been some of God's best surprises in your life?

Plans and Possibilities *(Joseph and Benjamin)*

- When have you felt God had a plan for something in your life? How did it work out?
- If you think that somehow God has plans for things, how does it make you feel: comforted, intimidated, confused, or...?

Torah Talk *(Moses)*

- What has been your perception of God's "law" over the years? How has it changed?
- How might you paraphrase the ten commandments?

Running from God *(Elijah)*

- When have you tried to run from God? What happened?
- Where have you heard God's voice?

Surprised by Healing *(Naaman)*

- How do you understand healing? How does God respond to prayer?
- When might you be inclined to resist God's message because the vehicle seemed too simple, or inappropriate, or insignificant?
- When has God intervened in your life to shatter your presuppositions?

Talking with Mother *(Hosea)*

- How do you resonate with this image of God? What is your experience of God as parent?

- When have you felt punished by God? When have you felt forgiven? How have you understood God's unconditional love?
- If you were interviewing God, what questions would you like to ask?

Star Followers *(The Magi)*

- Who do you think the magi might have been? What sort of people do you imagine them to be?
- What does it mean to you that foreigners or outsiders came to worship the Christ child?

Magnificat

- How much do you think Mary truly understood of her unique position and status?
- What else do you think Mary and Elizabeth might have discussed during their time together?
- What kinds of things do you think Mary and Joseph might have discussed as they planned for the birth of Jesus?

A Child Is Born

- How important to you are the details of the Christmas story? What happens to you emotionally when some of the details change?
- How does the story change for you if you think that Joseph and Mary were probably turned away not by complete strangers but by extended family? How does the story change for you if we understand that they were probably not "turned away" as we might understand it, but simply not given the best rooms?

John the Baptist and the Brood of Vipers

- How does your sense of this story change if you hear John's tone of voice differently?

- What do you think is the central point of John's message? What sort of things would John say if he were preaching in your community today?

That Preacher *(John the Baptist)*

- If you went out to hear John the Baptist preach, what question might you want to ask him? What answer do you think he would give?

- What is some of the chaff in your life that you would like Christ to remove? Write it on paper, and tear it up in little bits and toss it away. Turn around, as a symbolic act of repentance, and pray for God's guidance in starting over.

Dear Jesus *(Temptations in the Wilderness)*

- How readily do you relate to the temptations that Jesus faced in the wilderness?

- How might you apply those temptations to your daily living?

Herod's Letter

- When have you found yourself caught in a string of events that you felt you could not get out of, even when you wanted to? What did that feel like?

- When have you wished you could turn back time and undo something you had done? How might God help you come to terms with that?

- When have you offered up the truth of something you have done to God, and felt forgiven?

The Prodigal, part 1

- What has been your experience of welcoming someone home, or of being welcomed?

- Reflect on the image Jesus presents in this parable of God rushing to welcome us, rather than merely waiting. How does this change your perception of God?

Prodigal, part 2

- When have you celebrated being the recipient of God's grace?
- When have you been bothered by someone else receiving God's grace? What did you do about it? How did things turn out?

Two World Leaders *(The Pharisee and the Tax Collector)*

- Reflect on your nation or community. For what can you honestly give thanks? For what do you need to ask forgiveness?
- Try rewriting this piece in the context of your own nation or community, using specific issues and world events.

Crowd Conversion *(Zacchaeus)*

- When have you been judged wrongly by others, when you knew you didn't deserve it? What did that feel like?
- When have you felt forced to compromise principles? What did you do?
- When have felt challenged by God to change your view of others? What was the process? What changed in you because of that?

After the Wedding *(Jesus and Mary)*

- What kind of an image do you have of Mary, Jesus' mother?
- What have you imagined about Jesus' relationship with his parents, or other family members?
- Reflect on Jesus as a young person, beginning his ministry, having doubts and queries. How does this help you in your own faith journey?

Pilate's Report *(Holy Week)*

- Imagine that you have never heard of Jesus before, and your first awareness of him is the story of his arrest and trial. What impression of him do you form?

- The dramatic encounter between Jesus and Pilate emphasizes the confrontation between two views of power and authority. How do you live each day with the tension between Jesus' understanding of power, and the world's, as represented by Pilate?

- When, like Pilate, are you tempted to take the easy way out? What stops you?

Mary Magdalene's Legacy

- What have you heard, learned, and known about Mary Magdalene over the years?

- How have you understood her treatment at the hands of the church and historians?

- What would Mary Magdalene say to you, if she were speaking directly to you?

Included *(Philip and the Ethiopian Official)*

- What has been your experience of exclusion and the church—either being excluded yourself, or of knowing of others being excluded?

- Reflect on the words—attributed to St. Augustine: "I searched and searched and searched and searched, and finally God found me."

- What part can you play in making the church a place of radical inclusion?

The Sin Thing *(Romans 7 and 8)*

- How helpful for you is the image of sin as the state of being distanced from God?

- What are some other ways that you have understood sin?

- How do you understand grace?

Dare to Love *(1 Corinthians 13)*

- Draw a line on a piece of paper, and divide it roughly into thirds. Let it represent your life until now, in three stages. In each, write or draw something that represents your understanding of God. How has it changed? What would you like to let go? What would you like to reclaim?

- Set out two or three (small, achievable) practical ways that you can love a little more each day. Invite God to help you do those. Be open to simple, child-like ways. Plan to change the world with little steps, not huge ones!

Lectionary index

For those who might want to link the stories in this book with Sunday worship, or lectionary Bible study, the following indices are provided as a rough guideline. A note of caution, however: the nuances of lectionary readings and the texts used as a basis of these stories means that they may not always be a perfect match—for example, the John the Baptist stories in this book, being paraphrases, may or may not "fit" with the specific John the Baptist lectionary readings you might be using on a given Sunday.

Revised Common Lectionary

Note: in the Season after Pentecost, this lectionary uses two "streams"—one is commonly known as semi-continuous, and the other as paired readings.

Sarah's Laughter—*Proper 6A, semi-continuous; Proper 11C, paired*
Plans and Possibilities—*7th after Epiphany C; Proper 15A, semi-continuous*
Torah Talk—*Lent 3B; Proper 22A, semi-continuous; Proper 4B, paired*
Running from God—*Proper 14A, paired; Proper 7C, semi-continuous*
Surprised by Healing—*6th after Epiphany B; Proper 9C, semi-continuous; Proper 23C, paired*
Talking with Mother—*Proper 13C, semi-continuous*
Star Followers—*Epiphany*
Magnificat—*Advent 3A, Advent 4B, Advent 4C*
A Child Is Born—*Christmas*
John the Baptist and the Brood of Vipers—*Advent 2A, Advent 2C, Advent 3C, 1st after Epiphany C*
That Preacher—*Advent 2A, Advent 2C, Advent 3C, 1st after Epiphany C*
Dear Jesus—*Lent 1 A, B, C*
Herod's Letter—*Proper 10B*

The Prodigal, part 1—*Lent 4C*
The Prodigal, part 2—*Lent 4C*
Two World Leaders—*Proper 25C*
Crowd Conversion—*Proper 26C*
After the Wedding—*2nd after Epiphany C*
Born Again?—*Lent 2A; Trinity B*
Pilate's Report—*Palm/Passion Sunday; Good Friday*
Mary Magdalene's Legacy—*Easter A, B, C*
Included—*Easter 5B*
The Sin Thing—*Proper 9A, Proper 10A*
Dare to Love—*4th after Epiphany C*

Creation Spirituality Lectionary

This lectionary is available in my book Emerging Word: a Creation Spirituality Lectionary *published by iUniverse, April 2006. Available from online booksellers or at* www.emergingword.com.

Sarah's Laughter—*Epiphany 3*
Plans and Possibilities—*Transformativa 7*
Torah Talk—*Transformativa 13*
Running from God—*Epiphany*
Surprised by Healing—*Transformativa 24*
Talking with Mother—*Advent 2*
Star Followers—*Epiphany*
Magnificat—*Advent 4; Transformativa 14*
A Child Is Born—*Christmas*
John the Baptist and the Brood of Vipers—*Advent 2, Transformativa 13*
That Preacher—*Advent 2, Transformativa 13*
Dear Jesus—*Lent 2*
The Prodigal, part 1—*Easter 3*
The Prodigal, part 2—*Easter 3*
Two World Leaders—*Easter 4*
Crowd Conversion—*Transformativa 16*
After the Wedding—*Transformativa 18*
Born Again?—*Transformativa 15*
Pilate's Report—*Palm/Passion Sunday; Good Friday*
Mary Magdalene's Legacy—*Easter 2*
Included—*Transformativa 7*
The Sin Thing—*Epiphany 6*

Dare to Love—*All Saints' Day (not in book, but in updated material at* www.emergingword.com*)*

Roman Catholic Lectionary

US Conference of Catholic Bishops, 1998 edition.

Sarah's Laughter—*Holy Family B; 16th in Ordinary Time C*
Torah Talk—*Lent 3B*
Surprised by Healing—*28th in Ordinary Time C*
Star Followers—*Epiphany*
Magnificat—*Advent 3B; Advent 4B; Advent 4C*
A Child Is Born—*Christmas*
John the Baptist and the Brood of Vipers—*Advent 2A, Advent 2C, Advent 3C, 1st in Ordinary Time C*
That Preacher—*Advent 2A, Advent 2C, Advent 3C, 1st in Ordinary Time C*
Dear Jesus—*Lent 1 A, B, C*
The Prodigal, part 1—*Lent 4C*
The Prodigal, part 2—*Lent 4C*
Two World Leaders—*30th in Ordinary Time C*
Crowd Conversion—*31st in Ordinary Time C*
After the Wedding—*2nd in Ordinary Time C*
Born Again?—*Lent 4B*
Pilate's Report—*Palm/Passion Sunday; Good Friday*
Dare to Love—*4th in Ordinary Time C*

Scripture Index

This is a bit subjective—the stories are paraphrases and so their adherence to one or another version of a biblical passage is a matter of opinion.

About the author

Donald Schmidt fell in love with Bible stories while attending a combined Anglican/United Church of Canada Sunday School in his native British Columbia, Canada. This love of Bible stories continued through the pursuit of university degrees in comparative religion, theology, and finally a Doctor of Ministry in spirituality in 2006.

He has served as a minister in Quebec, New York, Vermont, and Hawai'i. In addition to parish ministry, Rev. Schmidt has written and edited church school curriculum, worship resources, and children's songs for over fifteen years.

He has taught church history, worship and preaching, and church dynamics at the Henry Opukaha'ia Center for Pacific Theological Studies. He recently published *Emerging Word: a Creation Spirituality Lectionary*, and is currently working on a series of daily devotional books based on Creation Spirituality.

When he isn't working in the church or writing, or walking on the beach, or knitting, or playing guitar, or traveling, he and his spouse spend their time "talking story" under the shade of their big mango tree.

For more information, visit www.emergingword.com.

978-0-595-40311-0
0-595-40311-5

Printed in the United States
56605LVS00006B